BURMA

A Socialist Nation
of Southeast Asia

WESTVIEW PROFILES
NATIONS OF CONTEMPORARY ASIA
Mervyn Adams Seldon, Series Editor

† *Japan: Profile of a Postindustrial Power*, Ardath W. Burks

Nepal: Profile of a Himalayan Kingdom, Leo E. Rose and John T. Scholz

Sri Lanka: An Island Republic, Tissa Fernando

The Philippines: A Singular and A Plural Place, David Joel Steinberg

Burma: A Socialist Nation of Southeast Asia, David I. Steinberg

Also of Interest

Burma's Road Toward Development: Growth and Ideology Under Military Rule, David I. Steinberg

Patterns of Change in the Nepal Himalaya, Mark Poffenberger

† Available in hardcover and paperback.

About the Book and Author

BURMA: A Socialist Nation of Southeast Asia
David I. Steinberg

Cut off from much of the outside world since the military coup of 1962, Burma has experimented with economic development schemes within a socialist context, transformed its political and constitutional structure, and continues to be besieged by rebellions – both ethnic and political, the complex heritage of a series of cultures that have interacted in ways too often only poorly understood. In this analytic introduction to Burma, Steinberg describes the diverse ethnic and geographic factors that have influenced the country, tracing Burmese history for the past thousand years with emphasis on the continuing themes that influence today's events. He looks at the colonial period and its effects on the political, social, and economic structure of postindependence Burma, then examines the civilian administrations and the causes of the military coup. His analysis of the military government's efforts to mobilize the nation politically, economically, and culturally, drawing on extensive field research, is current through 1981.

David I. Steinberg, at present with the U.S. Agency for International Development, lived in Burma for four years as assistant representative of The Asia Foundation. His books include *Burma's Road Toward Development* (Westview, 1981).

Mandalay – The Wall and Moat of the Royal Palace

BURMA

A Socialist Nation
of Southeast Asia

David I. Steinberg

Westview Press / Boulder, Colorado

Westview Profiles/Nations of Contemporary Asia

All photographs are from the author's collection. Map 3 is reproduced courtesy of the Library of Congress.

The views presented in this book are solely those of the author and do not necessarily represent those of the Agency for International Development or the U.S. Department of State.

Published in 1982 in the United States of America by
  Westview Press, Inc.
  5500 Central Avenue
  Boulder, Colorado 80301
  Frederick A. Praeger, President and Publisher

Library of Congress Cataloging in Publication Data
Steinberg, David I.
  Burma, a socialist nation of Southeast Asia.
  (Nations of contemporary Asia)
  "Westview profiles" – P.
  Bibliography: p.
  1. Burma.   I. Title.   II. Series.
DS527.4.S8   959.1   82-2590
ISBN 0-86531-175-7   AACR2

Printed and bound in the United States of America

To Ann Myongsook Lee,
who never knew Burma, but who one day may

Contents

Illustrations

Preface

Writing a short volume purportedly designed to provide the interested reader with a thorough grounding in all aspects of a single nation is an undertaking to be approached with considerable trepidation. It is especially onerous when that nation has a long and complex history involving not one, but a series of cultures that have interacted in ways that are still not completely understood.

The case of Burma is complicated both by the comparative paucity of material and by the questionable validity of much of the statistical information that exists. Basic current demographic data are lacking, and economic statistics are often dubious. Political decisions are not a matter of public record, and fieldwork by foreigners in the contemporary period has been and still is severely restricted. The press is controlled, much research by Burmese is classified, and information is closely guarded.

Other complications abound. There are comparatively few studies of Burma, and some of those done in earlier periods are subject to methodological problems of classic historiography—stress on dynastic materials and less emphasis on cultural and social dynamics. Some reveal strong prejudices, either from the colonial or Burman viewpoint. The Burmese have written, in Burmese and in English, less than might be expected on their own society and its dynamics both in the traditional and the contemporary periods. Burma is not a nation history obsessed, as are those in the Confucian tradition. Much remains unknown or simply surmised. More detailed anthropological and economic studies of the Burman and minority societies are especially needed.

These difficulties do not mean that analysis is impossible. The broad outlines of societal dynamics are often clear, if the details are sometimes obscured. Thus some of the conclusions and generalizations reached in this short volume are tentative. The book raises many issues, but if it excites interest in this country, generally neglected by the outside, and draws attention to its past and its potential, then an important purpose will have been achieved.

I would like to thank the publisher of Westview Press for giving me this opportunity to engage in one of my avocations—the study of Burma—and for assistance in the arduous process of editing. My special thanks go to Mervyn Adams Seldon, the editor of this series, and to Lisa DeGrazio, copy editor. I would like to express my appreciation to those who have read various drafts of this work: Jon Wiant, Michael Aung Thwin, Charles Smith, Ann Waggoner, and Cynthia Clapp-Wincek. They have improved its content and style immeasurably. I alone, of course, take responsibility for errors of fact or judgment.

I owe a great debt to many scholars, past and present, who have studied Burma and from whom I have freely borrowed. A few of their works are included in the Suggested Reading. To my many Burmese friends, both those made when I resided in Burma for four years and those met on subsequent trips, as well as those living in the United States, I give my thanks for your unconscious assistance. If this volume is at all sensitive to the Burmese scene, it is because of all of you.

David I. Steinberg

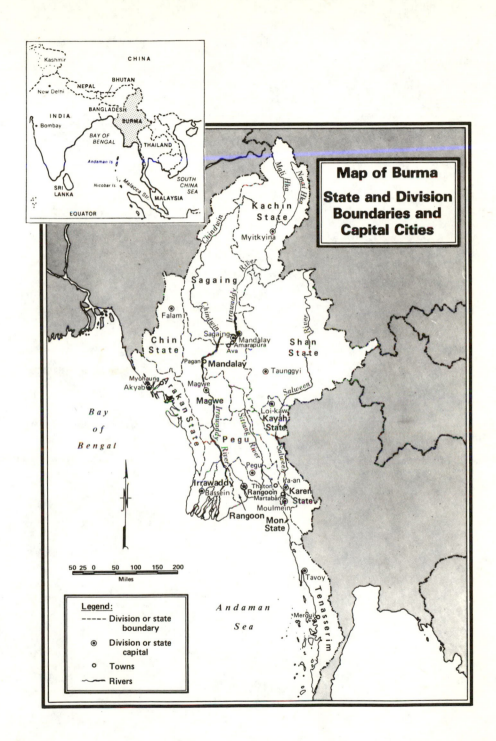

Map of Burma

State and Division Boundaries and Capital Cities

CHINA

Kashmir

NEPAL   BHUTAN

New Delhi

BANGLADESH   BURMA

INDIA

Bombay

BAY OF BENGAL

Andaman Is

SRI LANKA

Nicobar Is

Malacca Str

THAILAND

SOUTH CHINA SEA

MALAYSIA

EQUATOR

Mali Hka

Nmai Hka

Kachin State

Myitkyina

Chindwin

River

Sagaing

Irrawaddy

Chindwin

Falam

Sagaing   Mandalay
Amarapura
Ava

Chin State

Pagan   Mandalay

Shan State

Taunggyi

Salween

Myohaung

Magwe

Akyab

Arakan State

Magwe

Irrawaddy River

Bay
of
Bengal

Loi-kaw

Kayah State

Sittang River

Salween

Pegu

Pegu

Thaton   Pa-an

Irrawaddy

Bassein   Rangoon

Karen State

Martaban

Rangoon

Moulmein

Mon State

50 25 0   50   100   150   200
Miles

Tavoy

Andaman
Sea

Merqui

Tenasserim

Legend:

‑ ‑ ‑ ‑ ‑ Division or state
boundary

⊙ Division or state
capital

○ Towns

⁓ Rivers

1

The Physical and Social Environment of Burma

The vicissitudes of Burmese political life obscure the continuous, if not harmoniously interwoven, threads of Burmese history and culture. Kaleidoscopic changes have affected the Burmese polity for some 1,000 years. Dynasties have risen and fallen, rebellions have flowered and withered, centrifugal forces have pushed the Burmese beyond their boundaries, external pressures have brought foreign powers into Burma, and minorities have succumbed to Burman arms and risen again in insurrection. Burmese rule has been replaced by colonial authority, which in turn has evolved into renewed independence. Democracy has blossomed but been cut off by military autocracy. Revolts have permeated Burmese life, either to replace or restore a king, to fight for autonomy or independence, or to struggle for or against foreign domination.

Yet underlying these manifestations of change have been important historical continuities. If dynasties rose and fell, if political forms shifted, concepts of political power and authority remained singularly similar for a thousand years. If new ideas were introduced, they were weighed against a pervasive Buddhist faith, and the new political or intellectual concepts were sometimes expressed in the language of scriptures. A strong sense of ethnicity, of "Burmanness," has been a hallmark of Burman life since the twelfth century, but more persuasively with the onslaught of colonialism. The past has not only unconsciously pervaded the present, but the Burmans have consciously used it to legitimate the new.

Colonial rule introduced forces and inadvertently helped foster a resurgence of older concepts. The leitmotifs of the colonial experience were the search for a new and redefined Burmese identity, the development of nationalism, a resurgence of Buddhism, and the introduction of socialism and its general acceptance among leaders and intellectuals. These themes of the twentieth century were responses to colonial domination and the resultant economic and social changes – including

1

the spread of a money economy, Western law and real estate registration, land alienation, Christianity, and new avenues of both repression and mobility. Political nationalism was a natural response to British colonialism, but the growth of ethnic nationalism was also significant, giving birth to problems that continue to plague the nation. Buddhism became associated with nationalism as well as with the Burmese identity (as defined by the majority Burmans) and was invigorated by these alliances.

The geography of the country helped shape some of these ideas and affected the internal distribution of peoples and modes of agricultural production. It influenced Burma's relations with its neighbors and also helped mold Burmese history. Thus it is to the geographic setting of Burma that we must first turn before exploring Burmese history.

PHYSICAL CHARACTERISTICS

Burma is a land of geographic and ethnic diversity. Its particular longitudinal mountain ranges and rivers have affected the distribution of and relations among ethnic groups, as well as shaping the country's varied agricultural patterns. Its location north of the traditional monsoon-influenced maritime trade routes from southern India across the Bay of Bengal to the Isthmus of Kra and the Straits of Malacca kept central Burma – the heartland of the major ethnic group called the "Burmans" – relatively isolated from major international commerce before Western expansion. Mountainous borders, often splitting ethnic groups indiscriminately and creating diverse political allegiances, sheltered these peoples from stringent Burman control during the monarchy and limited trade overland with neighbors – China to the north, Thailand (Siam) to the east, and the subcontinent to the west. Although a deterrent to extensive commerce, Burma's inhospitable periphery did not completely block contact or trade, for even in Roman times emissaries went from Rome to Han dynasty China through Burma in A.D. 97 and A.D. 121. The natural barriers did not prevent invasions of Burma or Burmese attempts at expansion, nor did they discourage British efforts in the nineteenth century to exploit new trade routes or to explore development of a railroad to south China to compete with the growing French influence emanating from Indochina.

Shaped somewhat like a lopsided diamond, Burma is 676,552 square kilometers (261,217 square miles) or about the size of Texas. It extends over 1,930 kilometers (1,200 miles) from the northern Himalayan peak of Hkakabo (5,967 meters, or 19,578 feet) on the border of eastern Tibet to the tropical mangrove swamps of the lower Tenasserim region on the Thai frontier. Burma's borders are cartographical, not ethnic or economic. They total 5,102 kilometers (3,170 miles) and are, for most of their length, mountainous, shaped like a horseshoe encircling the Burman homeland. To the east, running north, a longitudinal range of mountains covers the length of the Tenasserim Division and Karen State boundaries, demarking the Thai border, a total of about 1,800 kilometers (1,118 miles). There are few passes in the Karen and Tenasserim regions, but one of the most important is the Three Pagoda Pass, which provides convenient access from Lower Burma onto the rice plains of the Bangkok region.

Continuing around the horseshoe to the north, we come to the Shan plateau, a section of rolling hills and mountains rising from a plain of about 1,000 meters (3,280 ft.). To the south, the Shan plateau borders Thailand; to the east, the Mekong River borders Laos for 238 kilometers (148 miles); and to the north lies China. The plateau is bisected by the generally unnavigable and swift Salween River, rising in Tibet and debouching in the Gulf of Martaban near Moulmein. Only the lower 120 kilometers (75 miles) are navigable, giving boat access to Paan, the capital of the Karen State.

The arc of mountains continues north, forming the boundary, long disputed, between the Burmese Kachin State and the Chinese province of Yunnan. The total length of the China-Burma border is 2,185 kilometers (1,358 miles). The horseshoe reaches its apex in the high Himalayas near eastern Tibet. Moving south along the range on Burma's western frontier are spurs, the Naga and Chin hills on the Indian frontier. Actually mountains, they rise over 3,000 meters (9,842 feet), ending in the Arakan Yoma ("hills") at the Bay of Bengal. The Naaf River provides a short border of 72 kilometers (45 miles) with Bangladesh.

The Arakan Yoma is made up of relatively low mountains of 1,000 meters (3,280 feet), covered by dense jungle and sparsely populated. Historically it shielded the coastal Arakanese plain from final Burman domination, although not from forays and hegemony, until 1784. Its position prevents the southwest monsoon, moving in from the Bay of Bengal from the end of May until October, from dropping much rain on central Burma. Rainfall on the Arakan coast is generally over 5,000 millimeters (200 inches), but north of the Arakan Yoma in central Burma it may be as low as 500 millimeters (20 inches), concentrated in four to five months. The coastline of Burma is 2,655 kilometers (1,650 miles) from Bangladesh to the Thai border.

Between these eastern and western mountains and plateaus lies the heartland of Burma. It is composed of two river-valley systems: the Irrawaddy and its tributaries to the west and the shorter Sittang to the east. These valleys are split by a range of hills called the Pegu Yoma, the northernmost peak of which is the 1,519-meter (4,984-foot) Mount Popa in central Burma, an extinct volcano and the reputed home of some of the Burmese *nats* ("spirits"). Close to the coast, the hills become less pronounced, ending in a small prominence that forms the base of one of the most important and revered centers of Buddhist pilgrimage, the Shwedagon Pagoda in Rangoon. The Pegu Yoma is heavily forested throughout most of its length and, until the past two decades, provided no lateral communications in its central portion between the vast Irrawaddy River valley to the west and the smaller but important Sittang River valley to the east. It was the site of much insurgent activity in the early years of the republic.

The Sittang River rises in central Burma south of Mandalay and is fed from runoff from the Shan plateau to the east and the Pegu Yoma to the west. It flows south to the Gulf of Martaban. Due to deforestation, it has badly silted during this century. In its middle reaches lies the city of Toungoo, the origin of one of the three dynasties that unified Burma.

The Irrawaddy to the west of the Pegu Yoma is the main artery of Burma — Kipling's "Road to Mandalay" — and the entrance as well to north Burma. Originating at Burma's northernmost frontier on the borders of eastern Tibet, it flows south through the Kachin State. In Burma Proper, it is joined southwest of Mandalay by its major tributary, the Chindwin, which flows south through a valley that demarks the border of the Chin and Naga hills to the west. The Irrawaddy effectively bifurcates the nation and is bridged at only one site, Ava-Sagaing, just south of Mandalay. It has been the major transportation avenue in Burma and drains over half the total area of the country. It is navigable for 1,450 kilometers (900 miles) in the dry season from the sea to Myitkyina (literally "near the big river"), the capital of the Kachin State, and to Bhamo 250 kilometers (155 miles) south of Myitkyina. Bhamo was the traditional staging area for the mule caravan traffic from Burma to Yunnan Province in China. The Chindwin is navigable for 610 kilometers (380 miles) north from its confluence with the Irrawaddy.

Burma has extensive forests, ranging from conifers above 1,500 meters (4,900 feet) to lowland mixed jungle and tropical rain forests of dense bamboo in some coastal regions. Individual teak trees occur in mixed growth in about one-quarter of all forests. Burmese records list forests as covering about 57 percent of the country. This figure is suspect, however, as it has remained unchanged for four decades. During this time, the population has grown and the ubiquitous practice of swidden (slash-and-burn) agriculture by tribes in mountain regions has denuded many of the hillsides. Besides forests, Burma has over a thousand varieties of orchids, some of which flower in pine trees in the Chin Hills at higher elevations. It has extensive fauna, including elephants, tigers, leopards, and the mithan, a type of wild buffalo used for ceremonial purposes among some tribes. The Arakan Yoma is one of the last remaining homes of the Asian rhinoceros. There are fifty-two varieties of poisonous snakes, about half of which are land species incuding cobras, kraits, and vipers. Burma has the highest death rate from snakebite of any country in the world.

Burma traditionally has had two distinct forms of agricultural production: wet-rice cultivation in the lowlands and *taungya,* a dry-cultivation method of the highlands. The distinction between the two is less one of ethnicity than of geography. Either fed by the monsoon or irrigation or both, wet rice requires extensive labor but generally produces an agricultural surplus. It sometimes may be replaced or supplemented by cash crops, either food or fiber. It is cultivated by the Burmans, Mon, Arakanese, Shan, and some of the lowland Karen. *Taungya* may be of dry rice, corn, or millet. Among some tribes, crops are produced by swidden, under which hillsides are burned, planted, harvested, and then left fallow for extended periods. Ecologically, it is a sound, productive system. As population has grown, however, a shorter fallow period has become necessary, thus depleting fertility and causing erosion. *Taungya* rarely produces any major food surpluses; however, it makes possible the major export smuggling of opium. This commodity, although illegal for two decades, is grown extensively in the Shan and Kachin states.

ETHNICITY

The central Irrawaddy plain encompasses the area of the traditional home of the Burmans, the major ethnic group in the nation. They comprise perhaps two-thirds of the total population of some 34 million in 1980. They are the only politically significant group whose total number resides within the present borders of Burma. The Burmans, belonging to the Tibeto-Burman linguistic family and speaking Burmese as their primary language, may have migrated south from western China and entered central Burma, perhaps from the Shan plateau, sometime before the ninth century A.D. Their migration may have resulted from or been accelerated by the upheavals associated with the consolidation of Nanchao, a kingdom with strong Thai and Lolo elements centered at Tali in what is now China's Yunnan Province. The similar Thai southern expansion and the creation of the kingdoms of Thailand may have been associated with the fall of Nanchao to China in A.D. 1253. The Burmans gradually replaced or absorbed another Tibeto-Burman group, the Pyu, who occupied the central Irrawaddy valley and left important monuments at Hmawza, near modern Prome. The origins of the Pyu are not known, but remains at Beikthanomyo ("Vishnu City") and Halingyi (in central Burma) dating from about the beginning of the Christian era are attributed to the Pyu. Chinese T'ang dynasty (A.D. 618–907) records comment favorably on the high level of culture among the Pyu in the seventh century. The Pyu were subjugated by Nanchao in the early eighth century.

The Burmans built their first and greatest capital at Pagan (849–1287) on the banks of the Irrawaddy. The remains of a myriad of pagodas of that period are one of the world's major archaeological treasures. Successive capitals were built north of Pagan on or near the river at Ava, Sagaing, Amarapura, and finally at Mandalay, all within a few kilometers of each other. They controlled the militarily and economically strategic region of central Burma at the bend of the river where it shifts west before continuing its southern flow.

If the central Irrawaddy plain was the locus of traditional Burman life, the Irrawaddy Delta, expanding at a rate of three miles per century, became one of the richest rice-producing lands in the world after the British annexed the region following the Second Anglo-Burmese War of 1852. Burman migration south to take advantage of this development was significant. Economic and administrative power shifted to Rangoon and the delta, but the central Irrawaddy plain retained its importance and remains today the traditional cultural core of Burman life.

Burma Proper was the provenance of the Burmans, but the peripheral areas in the arc around the Irrawaddy and Sittang valleys, including the coastal regions, were the homes of minority groups, who composed perhaps one-third of the total national population. Although accurate statistics are lacking, these groups are now probably more numerous. Speaking over 100 distinct languages, these peoples are bewildering in their diversity. Heterogeneous and politically divided tribes, such as the Lisu and the Akha, subsist on swidden agriculture and wield marginal political and economic influence, except through the opium trade. Others, such as the Shan, have evolved sophisticated political and social systems, some of a feudal nature. Historically, Burman interaction with minorities, with the important exception of the Mon, was not central to the Burman monarchy. A lack of nationhood, poor communications, and long distances from the court or administrative centers enabled minorities to live in traditional ways while submitting to the suzerainty of the Burman kings. Tension nevertheless developed in some border regions.

Of these groups, the Shan have been politically the most autonomous and organizationally the most sophisticated. Related to the Thai and the Lao, speaking a Thai dialect, and Buddhist by religion, they occupy the Shan plateau. There they established thirty-three separate states, each ruled by a *sawbwa* ("prince" or "maharaja"), with varying degrees of real or titular autonomy from the central court. The present

BURMA
Ethnic Groups

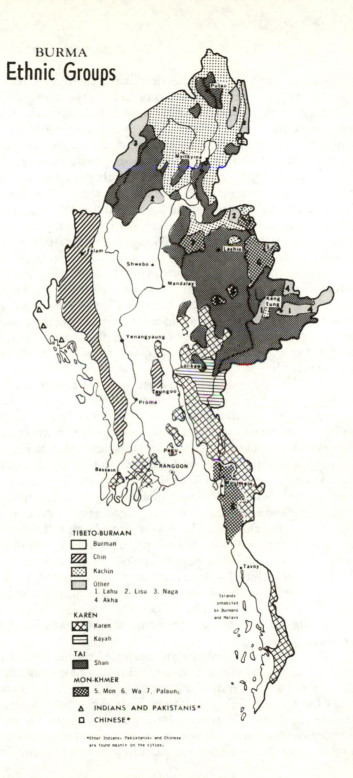

TIBETO-BURMAN

Burman

Chin

Kachin

Other
1. Lahu 2. Lisu 3. Naga
4. Akha

KAREN

Karen

Kayah

TAI

Shan

MON-KHMER

5. Mon 6. Wa 7. Palaung

△ INDIANS AND PAKISTANIS*

◻ CHINESE*

*Other Indians, Pakistanis, and Chinese
are found mainly in the cities.

Islands
inhabited
by Burmans
and Malays

Shan State, composed of the territory of these thirty-three substates and the Wa State, comprises about 20 percent of the land area of the nation, but only about 10 percent of its population. After the fall of the first unified Burman kingdom to the Mongols in 1287, the Shan expanded and controlled central Burma for about two centuries, creating small principalities as far away as the Chindwin, where they are known as the Hkamti Shan. There are substantial numbers of Thai and Shan in Yunnan Province, where the Chinese have established an autonomous area for them. The 1931 census, the last to publish ethnic and linguistic data (the census materials for 1941 were destroyed in the war, those for 1953 were solely urban, and the published data for 1973 reveal only geographic distribution, not ethnicity), lists 1 million Shan speakers. The total population of the Shan State in 1973 was calculated at 3.1 million, of whom perhaps half was Shan. The Shan have a strong hierarchical society with traditional authority vested in the *sawbwas*, who, up until 1959, retained title in name at least to all the land of their domain. They continued to exert some authority through the colonial period, but were stripped of their political, if not social, roles by the military caretaker government in 1959.

North of the Shan are the Kachin, a Tibeto-Burman people whose southern waves of expansion were the most recent in the successive movements of this linguistic group from their bases in western China. Resilient hunters, practitioners of swidden agriculture, and organized into extended clan systems, their push south and east was stopped only by British occupation of north Burma following the third, and last, Anglo-Burmese war of 1885-1886. Never unified politically, the Kachin evolved two (some say three) distinct political systems—the *gumlao*, democratic and egalitarian, and the *gumsa*, aristocratic and stratified and based on a Shan model. There was considerable fluidity between the systems. In the 1950s, the Kachin population was estimated to be from 350,000 to 400,000. The population of the Kachin State in 1975 was 765,000, but included a large number of Burman and other groups. The Kachin population in Burma today is unknown, but it is probably well over 500,000. There are also large numbers of Kachin in China. Most Kachin are animist, but a significant number have been converted to Christianity.

The western mountains are occupied by the Chin tribes and the related Naga to the north. Both are animists and members of the Tibeto-Burman linguistic family and have sizable populations on the India side of the border. The Chin speak some forty-four related languages and call themselves Zo (as the related Mizo people are known in India). They practice swidden agriculture and, at least until the beginning of this century, engaged in tribal warfare, including slave raids. The Chin State had a population of 281,000 in 1974, virtually all Chin. In 1931 the Chin, including those resident in the Arakan Hill tracts and the Irrawaddy Division, totaled 344,000. The Chin today may be undercounted and may actually number between 500,000 and 700,000. The total Chin population in both India and Burma may reach 2 million. A significant portion is Christian. There are no accurate statistics on the number of Naga in Burma (although estimates suggest 90,000 in 1957), but they totaled some 360,000 in India, the center of their influence, during the 1960s. They have achieved a certain international notoriety because of their rebellion against the Indian government.

The Karen are a large and heterogeneous series of tribes, the linguistic affiliations of which are still disputed. They include related peoples such as the Kayah (formerly called Karenni), the Pa-O, and the Padaung, the famous "giraffe" women of Burma. Composed of eleven groups, the Karen all together are the largest single minority in Burma, perhaps 10 percent of the population. The Karen proper are segmented into three dialect groups—the Sgaw, Pwo, and the less numerous Bwe—and are scattered throughout the eastern reaches of the country and the Irrawaddy Delta. They have had foreign visibility because of extensive conversions to Christianity, partially through the efforts of the American Baptist Mission, and during the British period had a prominent administrative role. Because many learned English in mission schools, about 22 percent of the Rangoon University student population during the 1920s was Christian Karen. In 1931 the Karen numbered 1,340,000, but today they may be close to 3 million. The Karen State population in 1975 was 895,000. There are about 200,000 Karen in Thailand. The Pa-O branch of the Karen linguistic community resides in the southern Shan State and is Buddhist. Estimates place their population at about 200,000 in 1970.

The Arakanese, a group speaking an older dialect of Burmese, were long protected from Burma Proper by the forbidding Arakan Yoma, where villages were until recently still stockaded to guard against tigers. They turned seaward, controlling at various periods the coastal piracy of the northern Bay of Bengal. Subjected to strong Indian and Hindu influences, they had important and independent kingdoms first at Vesali in the early centuries of the Christian era (until 1018) and then at Myohaung (1433–1784). The Arakan State population was 1,786,000 in 1975. There are a considerable number of Muslims in the region, some of whom, known as Mujahids, revolted early in the independence period. The number of Muslims today is unknown (it was 4 percent in 1931). Approximately 200,000 (presumably Muslims) fled to Bangladesh in 1978 in the wake of a Burma army alien registration drive, only to return later. Thus, it is assumed that Muslim migration into the Arakan during the

Bangladesh war for independence was significant. The Muslims today may compose up to 20 percent of the Arakanese.

Historically, the Mon are of special significance. The Burmans assimilated important elements of their culture from the Mon and waged many of their internal wars over control of this group. With Austro-Asiatic linguistic origins, the Mon are linguistically closer to the Khmer of Kampuchea (Cambodia) than to the Burmans. In the pre-Burman period, they occupied the southern part of what is now Thailand and the southern Salween and Sittang valley areas. The Mon may have introduced irrigated agriculture to the Burmans. They had major cultural centers first at Winka, then Thaton, and later at Pegu, where early European contacts were first made. The latter two were ports but have silted up. From the Mon, ardent Buddhists, the Burmans received Theravada Buddhism and a script, which they lacked. The long literary tradition of the Mon is still evident in Burma.

In 1931, the Mon numbered 337,000. Today, they may be close to 700,000, but because there has been much intermarriage with the Burman community, ethnic Mon are probably significantly fewer. The population of the Mon State in 1975 was 1,371,000. This figure includes Moulmein, however, the third largest city in Burma, which has a significant Burman population. There is a small Mon minority in Thailand, which has also been absorbed to a major degree.

Scattered among these major ethnic groups are less well-known peoples, including a few with sizable populations. Some, such as the Wa, numbering some 325,000 in 1946, are of more ethnographic than historical importance. Until recently, they practiced head-hunting for fertility rituals. Their territory, along the China border in the Shan State, has gained significance as the present base of the Burma Communist party. The more sophisticated Palaung (some 139,000 in 1931), who live in the northern Shan State and control the tea production of that region, were among the earlier inhabitants of what is now Burma. They are Buddhist and speak Austro-Asiatic languages. Other peoples are scattered throughout the hills, stratified by altitude rather than by region. The Lisu, the Lahu, and the Akha are among the more important.

Relations among the minority peoples and between the minorities and the Burmans have been varied and complex. Historically, the minority groups rarely lived in complete isolation and relationships were not static. Most peoples to some degree developed symbiotic relations with others and with the Burman majority. There was a certain amount of ethnic specificity in production, and interethnic trade was important. The ubiquitous five-day bazaars, which are still a feature of up-country life, brought diverse peoples together to trade their goods for what they could not produce. For example, the Karen used for ceremonial purposes large bronze drums made by the Shan, who did not use them.

Most minorities as such were peripheral to Burman interests except as they controlled key geographic regions—the Kachin-dominated trade and military routes to China, convenient invasion routes through the Shan states to northern Siam, or the Chin passes to Manipur. Conflict over the control of Mon territory in lower Burma, however, was a dominant theme of Burmese history. Minority social or political institutions, except for those of the Mon, had little impact on the Burmans. Some internecine warfare and slave raiding existed between the Chin and Burmans, for example, but there is little evidence of major intraethnic slaughter. In a sparsely populated region, people were more important than territory.

FOREIGN CULTURAL INFLUENCES
AND MINORITY RELATIONS

Burma was at the confluence of Indian and Chinese cultures and was a communications route between the two. Ethnically, most Burmese are more closely akin to the Chinese than to the Indians. Except for some Indian influence among the Arakanese, and a few remaining Salong—sea gypsies—who are Negrito, in the extreme southern islands off Mergui, all Burmese are racially Mongoloid. Chinese influence in Burma has been far less than in Indochina, however. Chinese control over the borders and the Burma frontier area was retarded by the persistence of the non-Chinese kingdom of Nanchao until the middle of the thirteenth century. Although the Mongol Yuan dynasty (1206-1368) subdued Yunnan, it was not until the Ming dynasty (1368-1644) that a Chinese presence there was firmly established.

However, Chinese penetration of northern Vietnam took place over a thousand years earlier and was essentially continuous, if not without friction. Burma was too far from major Chinese sources of power, and most Chinese invasions were mounted from Yunnan under local leaders. Four Chinese invasions from 1765 to 1769 under the Ch'ing dynasty (1644-1911) failed. Moreover, widespread and virulent malaria in the border river valleys effectively halted the movement of rice-growing Chinese settlers from Yunnan into these regions. Thus Vietnam adopted the Chinese concepts of kingship and bureaucracy and was strongly influenced by the Chinese language, whereas Burma did not adopt these institutions and was influenced by Pali, the Indian language of the Buddhist scriptures.

Culturally, the influence of India was paramount. Buddhism, originating in India but revitalized through Sri Lanka (Ceylon), had a power-ful and pervasive effect on Burmese life. It is now the religion of 85 percent of the population and of 99 percent of the Burmans. Indian ar-chitecture was the early model for Burmese monumental art. The Indian concepts of kingship, rather than the Chinese Confucian bureaucratic state, formed the basis on which Burman kings ruled. Burmese script is of south Indian origin. Burmese food—essentially Burma is a curry culture—is closer to the Indian than to the Chinese. Astrological and medical concepts are Indian in origin. In spite of the importance of these Indian influences, however, they were grafted onto a Burmese base that sometimes transformed them. The Indian caste system, for example, never caught on in Burma as it did in Sri Lanka. The status of Burman women was significantly higher than that of women in either India or China. The Burmese spirits were incorporated into the popular Buddhist pantheon.

Military contact with the Indian states, however, was of marginal significance, except after the British conquest of Bengal, and then it was essentially limited to Manipur and Assam. The Manipuri sacked Ava once, and the Burmans reduced both Assam and Manipur to tributaries at various periods. Only in the first part of the nineteenth century, when the Burmese exploded into eastern Bengal and Manipur and confronted British power and expansionist colonial policy, did Indian relations assume major importance. These threats to British authority were the causes of the First Anglo-Burmese War of 1824–1826 and resulted in British annexation of the Arakan and Tenasserim.

In contrast, military contact with China was important to Burma. With the change of Chinese dynasties, a strong central Chinese govern-ment, or the flowering of Burmese power, each side attempted to assert control over the border regions, both with limited success. Even today, the long boundary with China still forces Burma to regard Chinese in-terests with special attention.

Although China was the suzerain state of Burma for much of Bur-mese history, and although Burma paid nominal tribute to China, Thailand dominated Burma's foreign military relations until the nine-teenth century. Struggle for control of parts of the Tenasserim region, and thus the transit stations for the Bay of Bengal–Gulf of Siam trade, was not finally resolved in Burma's favor until 1793. The development of other routes, the stemming of piracy, the growth of Singapore in the early nineteenth century, and the introduction of steam naviga-tion—allowing traders to ignore the monsoon—made the territory less important. Britain found after annexation that the Tenasserim did not pay for its administration. Burma succeeded at various times in conquer-ing parts of northern Thailand—including Chiangmai where some Burmese influence is still apparent – and parts of Laos. In 1767, after repeated efforts, the Burmese destroyed the Thai capital of Ayuthia. Subsequently, the Thai moved it first to Thonburi and then to Bangkok. Today the Burmese word for Thailand is still *Ayuthia*. This traditional enmity between two Theravada Buddhist neighbors has never been completely overcome.

Historically, both the Chinese and the Indian minorities were important in Burma, although the latter dominated. The Chinese entered Burma in pre-British days – some from Yunnan, spurred by the nineteenth-century disruption of the Panthay rebellion, and others, the vast majority, from south China by sea after the British conquest. There were some 350,000 to 400,000 Chinese in Burma before World War II. Indian migration produced more enduring and dire consequences for Burma (see Chapter 3). The Indian population of Burma was estimated at 800,000 in 1957, but has subsequently decreased.

Burman internal relations with ethnic minorities have been more important than foreign relations in both the traditional period of the monarchy and in the period following Burma's independence. Foreign historians have characterized much of Burmese history during the sixteenth and seventeenth centuries as incessant wars of ethnicity between the Burmans, based in the dry zone of central Burma, and the Mon, who dominated the coastal regions of Lower Burma, except for the Arakan. This ethnic dichotomy, however, has been exaggerated. The Burmans may have been more interested in control over the prime resource of the region – population – than in its ethnic identity. In a period when land was plentiful, administration weak, and population sparse, wealth was measured not in the area controlled, but in the numbers who could be subjugated and used to enhance the regime's economic power.

Ethnicity, nevertheless, was important. The crowning of a Burman king in Mon Pegu was a political and ethnic act designed to remind the local Mon population of Burman intent and power. The Shan *sawbwas* submitted to Burman monarchs, who also married Shan *sawbwa* daughters to solidify alliances. The traditional mold of relations could not alter to meet changing circumstances, however. The British piecemeal occupation of Burma effectively ended Burman-minority interaction, thus freezing relations in a premodern pattern. The hill areas in which the minorities resided (those regions that came to be known as the Kachin, Shan, Chin, and Kayah states and the Salween District, which was incorporated into the Karen State) were administered separately from the rest of Burma, thus allowing no new and more modern relationships to evolve between the Burmans and the minorities. As a result, both groups had little experience in mutual accommodation. This situation created a problem when independence from British rule thrust the Burmans and the minorities together in 1947 to negotiate a new concept in cooperation and to incorporate it into the constitution of that year. Colonial rule had eliminated traditional conciliation and, among the Karen, intensified existing tensions that soon were stretched to the breaking point. The postwar era may one day be recognized as a prolonged and painful period in which new majority-minority relationships evolved. The problem continues to be the most enduring one contemporary Burma faces.

During the nineteenth and early twentieth centuries, Burman-minority tensions were exacerbated by religious differences. The Burmans, Shan, Mon, and some of the Kayah, Pa-O, and Arakanese, as well as some members of other groups, were (and are) Buddhist and were generally impervious to Christian missionary activity. However, substantial numbers of animist Karen, Chin, and Kachin were converted to Christianity. Their conversion, coupled with the divisive British administrative structure, heightened differences between these latter groups and the Buddhists, especially the Burmans, who were politically dominant. As Buddhism became more closely associated with nationalism in the two decades before World War II, the gulf between the minorities and the Burman Buddhist culture widened. Buddhism became the most important element of Burman identity, and Burman identity became confused with Burmese needs.

British preference for the Christian Karen, who offered no political and little nationalistic threat to colonial domination, also created tensions that today remain unresolved. They were intensified by the Karen alliance with the British against the Japanese and, in the early period of the war, against the Burmans, who had hoped for independence and thus cooperated with the Japanese after they promised it. The organization of the Burma army also contributed to this ethnic split. Before 1940, the British recruited soldiers from the hill "martial races," effectively excluding the Burmans. In 1940, only 12 percent of the army was Burman.

BURMA'S POTENTIAL

Burma is the most favorably endowed of the nations of Southeast Asia. It has the most advantageous ratio of population to arable land in the region. Today, half of Burma's arable land is still uncultivated. Burma also has extensive natural resources. Before World War II, it was the leading rice exporter in the world and the only developing country to export both food and petroleum. Not only did it export oil, but tin, tungsten, lead, and antimony as well. Its jade was of the finest quality, much sought after in China. Its rubies were world famous. Even so, its mineral resources were barely tapped; much had not even been explored. Burma also held three-quarters of the world's teak reserves, and its offshore fisheries were virtually untouched.

This potential has never been fully realized. In the prewar period, Burma was a wealthy colony that paid for itself, but it was the virtual prototype of a colonial economy. Major commercial agricultural production and industry were in the hands of foreigners, both British and Indian. The industry that did exist was largely centered on the processing of raw materials. Major employment was in food processing, such as rice mills. Sawmills boosted teak exports, and oil refineries and mines accounted for most of the other major industrial infrastructure, which was in any case modest and employed relatively few, mostly Indians. In 1940, the total labor force in factories (employing more than 20 persons and using outside power sources) was 89,383 in 1,027 sites. Two-thirds were in rice mills, and one-third of all industrial workers were in Rangoon, with an additional 20 percent in its suburbs. There were few manufactured consumer goods, other than handicrafts, and even indigenous textile production was hard pressed by British and Indian imports.

World War II destroyed even this modest industrial base. Burma suffered more than any other Pacific nation except Japan. The oil industry was completely wiped out. One-third of all cultivated land went out of production as a result of the physical dislocation of the population, and much of that land quickly reverted to jungle. Rice mills and sawmills only regained their capacity years later. Burma received no reconstruction assistance. The physical destruction was intensified by the insurrections that plagued Burma soon after independence. These problems, together with later misguided policies, so lowered the standard of living that it did not reach 1940 levels until 1976. Even the 1940 standard of living may have been lower than that of the predepression period.

The policies that various Burmese governments, civilian and military, formulated were products of monarchical Burma, the colonial experience, the growth of nationalism, and the struggle for independence. Thus we turn first to history and then to the rise of Burmese nationalism to chart these influences on contemporary Burma.

2

Traditional Burma and the British Colonial Administration

The early stages of the Burmans' slow migration south from their original home in western China are obscure. Entering the Irrawaddy valley, perhaps from the Shan plateau, as late as the early ninth century, they eventually came into contact with three highly developed civilizations. The Burmans, less acquainted with irrigated agriculture and urbanization, learned from these groups.

In central Burma, the Pyu were scattered along the Irrawaddy plain for some 300 miles from Prome to north of present-day Mandalay. The Pyu, a Tibeto-Burman people possibly distantly related to the Burmans, had established a series of walled cities, built pagodas and palaces, and mixed Theravada and Mahayana Buddhism together with Hinduism. They were sophisticated urban dwellers. T'ang records note:

> The wall of his [the Pyu king's] city, built of greenish glazed tiles, is 160 *li* in circumference, with twelve gates and pagodas at each of the four corners. They know how to make astronomical calculations. They are Buddhists and have a hundred monasteries, with bricks of glass, embellished with gold and silver.

To the south the Mon had established their base at Thaton between the Sittang and Salween estuaries, but had built irrigation systems extending as far north as Kyaukse in Mandalay Division. In Arakan was the kingdom of Vesali. Its walled city and palace had just begun to be excavated in 1980. Other peoples certainly lived either scattered among or on the fringes of these kingdoms, both in the hills and on the plains. The Karen, in all likelihood, lived throughout the south and east, and a great diversity of peoples occupied the northern plateaus and mountains.

17

THE KINGDOMS OF BURMA

When the Burmans moved in force into the Irrawaddy area, it was into a power vacuum. The Pyu kingdom had been subjugated in 832 by the Thai-Lolo state of Nanchao in present-day Yunnan Province. Pagan was the first known center of Burman civilization. It was founded in 849, although Burmese legend dates its history from the second century. Located on a steep bank of the Irrawaddy, the Pagan kingdom incorporated nineteen villages within a walled area. Pagan commanded a wide plain on both banks of the river, and its strategic position gave it control over much of the dry zone of central Burma. It was close to Mount Popa, whose mystical importance in Burman spirit worship predates Buddhism, although it was about 80 miles (128 kilometers) from the surplus grain production of Kyaukse. Some 300 miles (580 kilometers) up the Irrawaddy from the sea, it was still accessible by boat; and as the dynasty progressed, there were extensive contacts with Ceylon and India.

The first major figure in Burman history was King Anawrahta, the first unifier of the state, whose reign lasted from 1044 to 1077. In 1057 he moved south and conquered Thaton, the Mon capital. Legend has it that he did so to acquire the sacred Buddhist texts, as the Mon were in close contact with Ceylon, one major seat of Buddhist culture. He transported the texts, together with King Manuha, his court, and some 30,000 inhabitants back to Pagan. The Mon, far more culturally sophisticated than the Burmans, dominated Pagan life for the next century. The Mon's Theravada Buddhism became the religion of the court, although earlier Tantric elements persisted as minor sects for some centuries. The Burmans evolved their script from the Mon, and stone inscriptions were in Mon in the early period of the dynasty. Pagodas and temples were built, and for a century the Mon architectural style dominated. Over the course of the next 200 years, thousands of temples and pagodas, large and small, were constructed. Most were built of stuccoed brick in a fervor of dedication that today remains a marvel. Some 2,500 remain, a few rising over 200 feet above the Pagan plain and the Irrawaddy, dominating the landscape. Pagan today is one of the three major archaeological centers in Southeast Asia (the others are Angkor in Kampuchea and Borobodur in Java, Indonesia).

The expansion of Burman interests and power was a principal endeavor of Anawrahta's successors, Sawlu (1077–1084) and Kyanzittha (1084–1112), who incorporated parts of the Tenasserim region into Pagan's domains. Kyanzittha started construction on the Ananda temple, perhaps Pagan's most famous temple and an architectural symbol of the cosmic world, which the builder aimed to control. He supported the restoration of the Mahabodi temple in India, Buddhism's most revered site. Kyanzittha also sent missions to China in 1103 and 1106.

The zeal with which Theravada Buddhism was adopted is evidenced in the remains of the thousands of pagodas, monasteries, and temples. They required enormous amounts of labor not only for their construction, but for their maintenance as well. Surplus agricultural production was necessary to feed those who built them. Pagoda slaves were required, and they were often obtained through war, the expansion of the empire, and the resultant subjugation of outlying peoples. As religious interest rose, not only did the king and his entourage donate land and build pagodas, but others further removed from the immediate court circle did so as well. Because lands to sustain individual temples or monasteries were donated, more land was taken out of circulation for tax purposes as more pagodas were built. The economic base of the state thus contracted. When King Narathihapate (1254–1287) took six years to complete the Mingalazedi Pagoda, the Burmese could remark, "The pagoda is finished and the great country is ruined."

As economic decay set in, other factors also contributed to dynastic decline and instability. The Burmans found no solution to the problem of dynastic succession and never devised an administrative system to prevent disorders upon the death of a king and to ensure continuity of rule. Rebellions of subjugated peoples, such as the Mon and the Arakanese, sporadically broke out, and with Burman expansion arrogance developed toward neighboring China.

However much the country was weakened economically, ultimately the Mongols brought an end to Pagan's glory. The Mongols came to power in China in 1206 under Genghis Khan. When Kublai Khan took over the throne, Mongol expansion penetrated the southernmost province of Yunnan and destroyed the Nanchao kingdom. The Burmans were defeated by local Chinese forces in northern Burma in the latter part of the thirteenth century, but it was not until the Burmans murdered Chinese envoys that the Pagan dynasty finally fell in 1287 to the Mongols. Pagan as a city continued for a few more years, and the Mongols maintained a garrison at Tagaung, north of present-day Mandalay, until 1303. The stage was set for the temporary preeminence of another of Burma's ethnic groups, the Shan, in central Burma and for the resurgence of the Mon kingdoms in the south.

As the Mongols established control over Yunnan, their presence pushed the Thai, who had lived in south China, further south into what was to become northern Thailand. At about the same time that the first Thai kingdoms developed there, the Shan in Burma, linguistic cousins of the Thai, moved west down from the Shan plateau to the Irrawaddy and into the political vacuum created by the fall of Pagan. As the Chinese, who had moved against the Shan in 1300 to no avail, withdrew from northern Burma, Shan influence expanded throughout central Burma. They founded Ava about 1364 or 1365 in the Burman heartland. Ava, however, was a Burman, not a Shan, city. In central Burma, the Shan governed as Burmans, establishing fictive hereditary ties to ancient Burman rulers, and wrote their inscriptions in Burmese. They thus set the precedent whereby unifying rule in Burma was in a Burman context. Shan dominance along the Irrawaddy forced Burman migration to the Sittang, where exiles founded the town of Toungoo, which was later to play a pivotal role in Burmese history. The Shan also moved beyond the Irrawaddy into what is now the Kachin State and to the Chindwin River. By virtue of their organized feudal political system, they were able to establish small kingdoms in the agriculturally productive minority valley areas of the west and north. Shan rule soon deteriorated, however, into a number of petty, warring states.

When Pagan floundered and the Shan began their ascendency in the dry zone, the Mon reasserted their influence in the south. In 1287, as Pagan fell to the Mongols, Wareru, son-in-law of the great king Ramakhamheng, ruler of the early northern Thai kingdom of Sukhot'ai, reestablished Mon power, based first at Martaban. In 1385, Razadarit, perhaps the greatest ruler of the Mon, became king in Pegu. With its access to the sea, Pegu flourished. With additional ports at Martaban and Bassein in the Irrawaddy Delta, the Mon kingdom prospered. Pegu exported rice to India and to Malacca, after the Portuguese seized the city in 1511.

The year 1511 is considered a landmark in Southeast Asian history. It is the point at which modern – that is, Western-influenced – history in the region began. The Portuguese expanded their power first to Goa in India in 1510 and then to Malacca a year later, establishing their early predominance in the area. By 1519, they were operating a trading station at Martaban. The Portuguese were not the first Westerners to visit Burma, however. A Venetian, Nicolo de' Conti, who returned to Europe in 1444, visited Arakan and traveled overland across the Arakan Yoma to Ava. He then proceeded down the Irrawaddy to Pegu. He was followed by two other Italians, Hieronomo de' Santo Stefano in 1496 and Ludovico de Varthema in 1502. (Marco Polo wrote of Burma, but never actually went.) Pegu greatly impressed the Europeans with its splendor. Western rivalry and intervention were thereafter to play a role in Burmese history.

The first explosion of Burman dynastic energy was in Pagan; the second emanated from Toungoo in the Sittang valley. The Toungoo dynasty (1486–1752) was founded by Minkyino (1486–1531), but it was his son Tabinshwehti (1531–1550) who expanded the new Burman empire. He captured the Mon port of Bassein in 1535 and Pegu in 1539. He went on to take Martaban in 1541 with the assistance of Portuguese mercenaries, who acted as gunners. Their descendants still live in villages near Shwebo. He then established his capital at Pegu, perhaps because it would promote his planned conquest of Ayuthia. His energies not yet dissipated, he first turned west and invaded the Arakan, but failed to conquer its capital, Myohaung. Turning his attention eastward to Ayuthia, he attacked in 1548. At stake was not only prestige, but also control over the eastern portion of the Bay of Bengal trade. He was, however, unable to subdue that kingdom. It fell to his son Bayinnaung (1551–1581) to complete that task.

Bayinnaung's exploits in expanding Burman power are unequaled in Burmese history. Crowned at Pegu, he captured Ava in 1555, permanently destroying Shan power in Burma Proper. He went on to make himself suzerain over the Shan states, unifying the Burman empire for the second time in history. He conquered Chiangmai, and twice, in 1564 and 1569, captured Ayuthia, removing some of its population to Lower Burma. His expeditions extended into Laos on several occasions, but with only limited success.

The lack of an effective administrative system, rapacious behavior, and nascent nationalism all prevented lengthy periods of peace within the kingdom. Peoples revolted in a welter of turmoil that seemed unceasing. At the same time as these expansionist efforts and rebellions, Western interest in Burma increased, indicating the possibility of very profitable trade not only between Europe and Burma, but also between India and Burma. Intra-European rivalry was mirrored in the east, especially in India, but in Burma as well.

As Bayinnaung's kingdom began to collapse under the strain of internal revolts and external troubles, the European powers became enmeshed in Burma's turmoil. King Nandabayin (1581–1599) attempted to conquer Ayuthia five times, but these expeditions generally were unsuccessful. The Thai, in fact, reversed the pattern, capturing Tavoy and Tenasserim in 1593, and then took Moulmein. These setbacks were followed by a series of internal rebellions. Arakan revolted in 1599 and seized the port of Syriam, on the opposite bank of the river from Dagon. (Dagon was later named Rangoon, "the end of strife," by Alaungpaya in 1756). The Arakanese installed the Portuguese Philip De Brito, a freebooter, as head of Syriam. He later married a daughter of the Portuguese viceroy of Goa and became king of Syriam in the viceroy's name. He alienated the Mon by attempting to convert them to Christianity and was eventually overthrown and killed by King Anaukpetlun (1605–1628) in 1613. Although Anaukpetlun attempted once again to expand the kingdom and did for a period incorporate Chiangmai as a province, the unified kingdom waned. It would take about a century and a half before Burma once again would be united.

The Portuguese came first to Martaban and then to Syriam. The British, as their role in the East expanded and as Portuguese power faded, founded a major center of influence on the eastern shore of the Bay of Bengal at Mergui in the Tenasserim. When the Thai attacked and recaptured it, some sixty Englishmen were killed. It was not until the latter part of the eighteenth century that Burma finally regained complete and continuous control over that region. The British also established a trading station at Negrais Island off the Irrawaddy Delta. It lasted until 1759, when the Burmese finally burned their fort. In 1635, the Dutch established their first factory in Burma at Syriam. They were joined by the British in 1647, but the British withdrew ten years later. The French, to expand their interests in the region and to supplement their strong position at the Thai court, also built dockyards at Syriam in 1729 and courted the Mon.

The end of the Toungoo dynasty came when forces from both the west and the south finally destroyed the Burman centers of power at Sagaing and Ava. The Manipuri raided central Burma in 1738, capturing Sagaing and later Ava. They were followed by the Mon, who, in 1740, once again revolted. The Mon conquered Ava in 1752.

The disintegration of a unified Burma was finally halted by the development of a new center of power emanating from Shwebo, a town north of Mandalay in the dry zone. There the last of the traditional unifying Burman dynasties, the Konbaung dynasty (1752–1885), arose. In this dynasty, the capital, though moved, was always situated in central Burma, near or on the Irrawaddy. The capital was first in Shwebo (1752–1765), then removed alternatively to Ava (1765–1783; 1823–1837) and Amarapura (1783–1823; 1837–1857), and finally situated at Mandalay (1857–1885). Alaungpaya (1752–1760) and his successors, Naungdawgyi (1760–1763) and Hsinbyushin (1763–1776), conquered all of Burma and then went on to subdue Manipur, Assam, parts of East Bengal, Laos, and Thailand. Alaungpaya signed the first treaty between Burma and a foreign power (England) in 1757. The treaty was not with the king of England, however, but rather with the British East India Company, which virtually controlled war, peace, and trade relations between England and Burma.

The Konbaung dynasty, like the two previous unifying kingdoms of Burma, pursued an expansionist policy whenever possible. It finally destroyed Ayuthia in 1767. So complete was the destruction that the Thai capital was moved south to the Thonburi area and then across the river

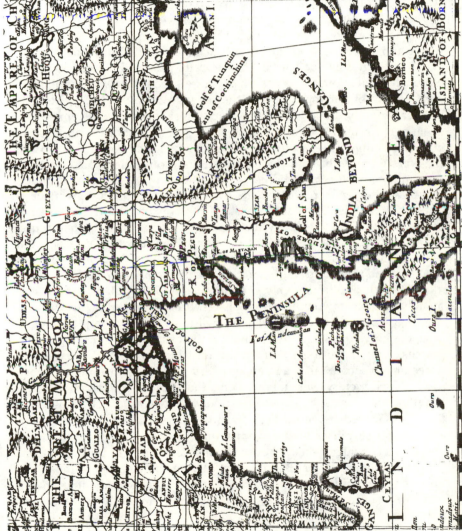

SOUTHEAST ASIA IN 1680

to Bangkok, where it has remained. Vientiane was captured. In 1770, even the Chinese were defeated and a peace treaty signed on the battle site. The Burmans attempted to pursue a vigorous offensive policy on the western frontier as well, but there it came into conflict with an equally expansionist British policy under the leadership of the East India Company. This confrontation led to the dismemberment and ultimate demise of Burma as an independent kingdom.

The expansionist policies of the Burman Pagan, Toungoo, and Konbaung dynasties need explanation. Questions are continuously raised about the aggressive policies of theoretically passive Buddhist societies, although similar questions are rarely asked about Christian nations, in part a result of a myopic view of the relevance of Buddhist precepts to political reality. The incessant imperialist wars were not solely economic, for many of the campaigns were directed at areas of marginal economic importance. Conversion was not the motivation, for most of the wars were with other Buddhist nations. Conversion was also not a determining factor in Buddhist history. According to popular myth, these campaigns were motivated by attempts to procure white elephants. White elephants are important symbols of an early incarnation of the Buddha, but it is likely their seizure was more effect than cause. Perhaps more important was the concept of the *cakravartan,* a Sanskrit term (*setkyamin* in Pali-Burmese) for the universal Buddhist emperor who pacified the world in preparation for the coming of the future Buddha. This idea had messianic connotations and may have been a role model for the last two unifying dynasties. It is also possible that the concept may have served to motivate or legitimize foreign conquest. In any case, the kings recreated the symbols of the cosmos in their temples and palaces, which were partially built for this purpose. Warfare was necessary to secure labor and an agricultural base for feeding the work force. Thus, victory was important for the shift of population that followed it. The Burmans removed relatively large numbers of people from their conquered territories to Burma, where they increased the agricultural surpluses of the country and helped build pagodas. Booty was also a consideration, and even the most sacred temples were looted for their gold and silver. Buddha images were transported to the court. Thus, a variety of factors, including pride and aggrandizement, probably played a role in the continuing and pervasive pursuit of expansionist policy.

BRITISH EXPANSION INTO BURMA, 1824-1886

King Bodawpaya (1781-1819) continued the military policy of his predecessors. He repeated the incessant Burman attacks on Thailand, but they were poorly conceived and unsuccessful. His major military victory was his expedition into the Arakan in 1782 and its final subjugation and annexation into the Burman kingdom in 1784. On the west bank of the Irrawaddy, north of Mandalay, he started building the Mingun Pagoda, a massive edifice that was to rise over 500 feet when completed. It was never finished in spite of seven years of arduous construction by thousands of laborers, many of whom died in the attempt. The demands for labor were so great that Arakan revolted in 1794. This revolt was but the first in a series that each time brought forth Burman retaliation, a flood of refugees fleeing into Bengal, and Burman demands that they be returned.

The British, however, were occupied elsewhere—with the French and with insurrections in parts of India and Nepal. They were not able to respond quickly to Burmese concern over the refugees and their raids back into Burma. Yet the British viewed their expansion into Southeast Asia as an important element in their efforts to control the potentially rich China trade and to deny that area to the French. The Burmans had little understanding of the power behind the East India Company and of the importance that the British placed on their position in Bengal, especially in the light of French rivalry. The British also depended on Burmese teak reserves as the prime source for their shipbuilding activities in the Bay of Bengal. To these ends, and to increase trade, the British sent emissaries to the court at Ava and tried to establish a resident there, but relations worsened.

When Manipur refused to recognize the suzerainty of Burma by sending officials to the coronation of the Burman king Bagyidaw in 1819, the Burmans invaded Manipur to reestablish its tributary relationship. The Manipuri forces and court fled westward into India, inflaming the frontier of British India and again disturbing Assam and Manipur. At this point, the British governor-general of India determined to invade Burma. The result was the First Anglo-Burmese War of 1824–1826. From a European viewpoint, it was probably one of the worst managed wars of the period. More foreign soldiers died from disease and heatstroke than from battle wounds. Some 15,000 of the 40,000 troops perished. The Burmans fought valiantly; but following the death in battle of the great Burman general Bandoola and the British advance into central Burma from Rangoon, which was taken quickly at the beginning of the struggle, the Burmans capitulated. The Treaty of Yandabo in 1826 ceded the Arakan and Tenasserim regions to the British and kept the Burmans out of Manipur and Assam, which the British eventually incorporated into their empire. A British resident was posted in the Burmese capital, Ava, and an indemnity was enforced on the Burman court.

The intervening years between the First Anglo-Burmese War and

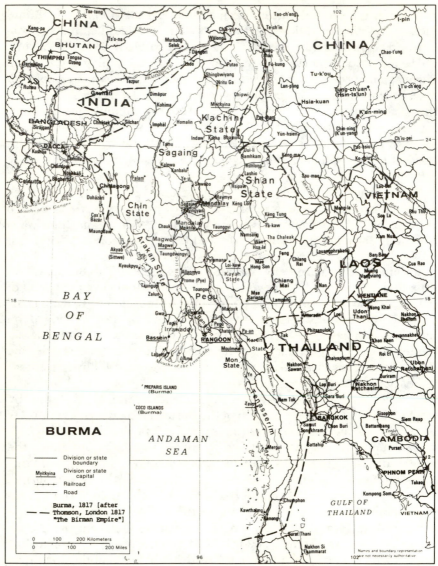

Base 503538 12-77 (543580)

the Second Anglo-Burmese War (1852) were a period of consolidation of British interests in occupied Burma and of dynastic decay in independent Burma, with deteriorating relations between the two. Arakan, because of its rice production, soon became very profitable to England. Akyab, its principal town, became a free port and soon was the third busiest in all of India. Tenasserim, from the British standpoint, was a loss. In Burma, two of the monarchs in this interwar period went insane. Under a system where there was no single, undisputed line of succession, new kings carried out bloody executions to eliminate all possible pretenders to the throne and their immediate followers and families, a practice that dismayed the British. Basically, there was conflict between the two cultural groups, neither of which had any real understanding of the norms and values of the other. Because the British would gain obvious geopolitical and economic advantages if they could link the Arakan and Tenasserim, by incorporating the territory of the old Mon kingdom in between, war was inevitable.

The British residency in independent Burma closed in 1840, as relations worsened. Finally in 1852, the British used a dispute between two British ship captains and local Burmese officials, in which the captains claimed unfair treatment, as a pretext to declare war. The Second Anglo-Burmese War lasted less than one year and was never officially ended. The de facto effect was the ceding of Lower Burma to the British: the Irrawaddy Delta, Rangoon, and the Mon territories of Pegu and Martaban. The war put a new and progressive king, Mindon, on the throne, but the inexorable drive of empire could not be stemmed.

The development of the Irrawaddy Delta as the premier rice-growing area of the world prior to World War II began after this annexation. Indian demand for Burmese rice was already evident, and Europe as well became more interested in this commodity as the American Civil War cut off U.S. supplies. The Burmans moved their capital to Mandalay in 1857. Mandalay was symbolically situated between Mandalay Hill, a religious site, and the Arakan Pagoda, the sacred image of which had been removed there on the Burman conquest of Myohaung in 1784. Intended to improve the fortunes of the dynasty, the move of the capital had no effect. Mandalay was cut off from the sea, and thus from most foreign contacts.

During his reign, King Mindon (1853–1878) attempted to carry out a number of administrative and other improvements, but the state could not cope with the internal and external pressures. The Karenni (Kayah) states rebelled; and in 1875, when the British refused to allow the shipment of arms to Mandalay, the Burmans were forced to recognize its independence. Emulating the early tradition of Buddhist monarchs, the able King Mindon held the Fifth Great Buddhist Synod in 1872, the first to be held in 2,000 years, to purify the Buddhist scriptures. The results can still be seen in Mandalay, where the texts were inscribed on marble slabs. He started a new pagoda before his death, one that a French architect estimated would take 5,000 men working full time 84 years to complete. He never finished more than the foundations.

The third stage in the British annexation of Burma was not too long delayed. The British were distressed by overtures from Mandalay to the French and especially excited by the prospects of a railroad from Burma to south China through Yunnan that would open that vast empire to British commercial interests. In British Burma, annexation of the Mandalay kingdom was in the air. The British held public expenditures in Lower Burma down because invasion of Mandalay was thought to be imminent and would require government funds. A dispute between the Bombay Burmah Trading Corporation and King Thibaw (1878-1885) over revenue and taxes from the royal teak concessions the company was exploiting was the excuse for, not the cause of, the Third Anglo-Burmese War (1885-1886). It lasted about a week. The king and his family were exiled to India. The last independent kingdom of the Burmans, which in its vicissitudes had lasted over a thousand years, fell.

King Thibaw attempted to modernize elements of his administration as had Mindon before him. However, no amount of change or progress, no internal acts by the throne, could have halted the acquisition of this remaining piece of the Southeast Asian imperial puzzle. The First Anglo-Burmese War was a conflict of cultures, of misapprehensions of intent and power. The second was a result of the geopolitical and bureaucratic need to link imperial possessions. The third war was more mundane: British commercial interests and Anglo-French rivalry made it inevitable. Burma was the "stricken peacock."

If the conquest of the kingdom of Mandalay was simple and almost bloodless, the pacification of that land was long and arduous. For over five years the British, using Indian troops and Karen levies, ranged across Upper Burma in a series of major campaigns. In the absence of a monarch, royal pretenders sprang up in various areas, viewing the fall of the dynasty as a portent of their own incipient royal status. The destruction of the monarchy led to widespread dacoity as traditional means of law and order broke down. Expeditions were sent throughout the north; the most extensive was to the Chin Hills, where a long campaign was fought to pacify the area. Troops occupied the Kachin hills and the Shan states. The Burmese fought, but it was sporadic and uncoordinated. They had no chance against a well-organized campaign and modern weaponry.

THE COLONIAL PERIOD, 1886–1948

Britain annexed Burma in 1886 not to England, but to India. Burma thus became one of the many provinces of British India, its individuality and unique needs ignored at the higher levels of adminstration. This decision was to have dire consequences for the Burmese. It led to administrative and management decisions based on the Indian model, as well as to the importation of Indians to staff the civil service and supply the manual labor for new occupations and industries that were introduced. The Burmese military was also structured on an Indian model that was irrelevant to Burma and indeed proved to be inimical to future harmonious relations among ethnic groups. New administrative forms followed conquest as well. The district was introduced and became the most important administrative unit. It was only eliminated in 1972. The function of the headman changed, and his authority was diminished. He came to represent the lowest level of a central bureaucracy, rather than the highest level of local administration. Burma was governed first from Calcutta and then from Delhi. The Indian Civil Service was the elite institution and did not admit Burmese for almost four decades after annexation.

The purpose of British administration was the maintenance of law and order and the collection of revenue. The formation of an extensive police system and the need for increased taxation led to the establishment of the British court system. As in India, the result was a proliferation of lawyers and paralegal functions that were very attractive to many Burmese. Extensive tax systems were devised, and Burma began, just a few years after annexation, to pay for itself. The corollary of a self-financed colony from the mercantile viewpoint was laissez-faire economics. Burma became a fertile ground for British investment and for Indian speculation as well. Even when conditions deteriorated, the government was loathe to intervene and support the impoverished elements of the population. The British spent more on police than on education and more on prisons than on health and agriculture combined. In spite of this, over time Burma became known as a country with one of the highest per capita crime rates in the world.

The British divided Burma into two sections: the area of Burma Proper where the Burmans were in the majority (it also included Arakanese and Mon regions) and the hill areas inhabited by other minorities. Burma Proper was administered directly, and old elites had no power there. The hill areas retained some of the traditional leadership under overall British supervision. These areas included the Shan states, the Karenni states (later called the Kayah State), the Kachin and Chin hills, and the Karen Salween District. The hill regions eventually came under the control of a separate frontier administration in 1922. The separation of the Burmans from the minorities was designed to protect the latter, but it limited interaction between both groups, thereby freezing majority-minority relations. This created tensions that were to come to a head after independence. The British were accused of following the familiar "divide-and-rule" policy. In fact, there was no need for them to do so, for Burma was already divided long before foreign conquest.

Nevertheless, this policy, in particular, had unfortunate consequences after the British left.

Local governance was slow to develop in Burma. When it did, it was confined to Burma Proper. Until 1897, Burma was governed as a province of India under a chief commissioner. After that date, the province was under the control of a lieutenant-governor, with an advisory council reporting to him. Although ruled from India, Burma was regarded as something of a stepchild. The Burmese were considered much less sophisticated than the Indians and so simple that they were unsuited for self-government. When the Minto-Morley reforms of 1909 were introduced into India and established legislative councils at the provincial level, which increased in size and had a considerable number of elected members, Burma lagged far behind. The Legislative Council in Burma was expanded from nine to seventeen, but only one member was elected. Moreover, the elected member was from the Burma Chamber of Commerce, a British preserve. In 1915, there were further reforms with modest increases in the council; twenty-eight were chosen by the government and two were elected, the second from the Rangoon Trades Association. British rule was controlled by the official British community in league with business.

In 1917, the Montagu-Chelmsford reforms increased self-government in India. They were not applied in Burma, however, because the British considered that the Burmese had no interest in self-government. This was a gross misreading of Burmese sensitivities; it piqued Burmese pride and increased the desire for self-rule. Reforms were introduced slowly in Burma. Under a new constitution of 1923, Burma had a legislature of 103, of whom only 9 were elected, the remainder being named by the government. Those elected were communal representatives; that is, seats were set aside for Indians, Anglo-Indians, and the Karen. Some 58 seats were reserved for Burmese and European constituencies. Ironically, in 1930, when the British finally recognized the need for separating Burma from India, the Burmese suspected that division would give them less autonomy than if they remained a part of India. In the elections of 1932, the antiseparatists won a majority. In 1937, however, based on the election of 1936, Burma was finally divorced from India. A two-chamber parliament was decreed. The Senate had half of its members nominated by the governor. The House of Representatives was completely elected under an extended franchise. Of its 132 seats, 22 were set aside for communal representation.

As Burma grew economically and as a modest effort began to bring a modicum of local government to Burma Proper, there were growing nationalist rumblings. They began to permeate intellectual life and spread throughout the country. They had their genesis in concern over Buddhism but became more widespread with disappointment over the 1917 Montagu-Chelmsford reforms. They soon centered among the students when a new university was proposed in 1920. Students wanted the university to be more representative of the mass of the population, not limited to elites. They boycotted the university, and the movement soon spread throughout the country. Monks agitated for independence, and intellectuals grouped together to destroy British social superiority and to demand self-government. They led strikes of workers and students, and concern over foreign domination centered on Indian economic exploitation as well. Yet traditional concepts of kingship, seemingly lost in the fervor of interest in new political systems, were still evident. They reached their apex in the Saya San Rebellion of 1930–1931.

The Saya San Rebellion was an important reflection of nationalism. Its rationale was indigenous, owing nothing to European intellectual fermentation or to the Indian movement for independence. It was rooted in traditional Burmese concepts of kingship. Saya San, a former monk and lay doctor, surrounded himself with the regalia of the traditional Burmese kings, including the white umbrella—an ancient symbol of divine kingship. He built a symbolic palace in the jungles of the Pegu Yoma, from which, at an auspicious hour, he launched his rebellion and crowned himself king. His troops, armed with traditional weapons and tattooed with magic symbols to make them invulnerable to guns, were known as the *galon* forces (i.e., garuda, a bird of South and Southeast Asian mythology). They planned to overcome the *naga,* the "serpent," a symbol of the British. More than 8,000 troops were required to subdue the rebellion, which was more virulent in areas hard hit economically by the depression. The British misunderstood the revolt's nationalistic origins and the contribution of deteriorating economic conditions to its spread. They credited its growth to the "restless and excitable" nature of the Burman and to the "incredibly ignorant and superstitious Burman peasantry." The rebellion was extinguished, and Saya San tried and hanged in 1937; but the memory of the rebellion was later revived and honored in the military period.

Burmese politicians during the short period of local government had considerable authority over some of the affairs of Burma Proper. However, defense, foreign affairs, and monetary policy were reserved for the governor. Burmese politics in this period was characterized by factionalism based on the personal following of several key leaders who assumed positions of importance in succeeding governments. They included Dr. Ba Maw, who founded the quasi-socialist Sinyetha ("Poor Man's party"); U Saw, who was jailed by the British during the war for suspected pro-Japanese leanings and executed in 1948 for planning the assassination of Aung San; and Sir Paw Tun, a conservative leader of the elite. Although there were ideological differences among these men, these concepts were subordinate to their personal ambitions and differing personalities.

As World War II broke out in Europe, the influence of Indian agitation for independence spread with increased intensity to Burma, which was supporting China in its fight against Japan by channeling supplies via the Burma Road. Aung San, the leader of the struggle for independence following the war, and twenty-nine other Burmans secretly left Burma and were trained by the Japanese. When war in the Pacific broke out, the "Thirty Comrades," as they became known, entered Burma with the Japanese forces. Burma was woefully unprepared for the onslaught, and the Japanese quickly occupied most of the country, cut the Burma Road to China, and offered the Burmese their reward for assistance in the "liberation" of Burma.

In August 1943, Burma was declared an independent country, and Dr. Ba Maw, who had escaped from British imprisonment, became the prime minister. Aung San became minister of defense and U Nu minister of foreign affairs. All were to figure prominently in Burma's future. At this time, Ne Win was a brigadier in the Burma Defense Army, set up under Japanese auspices.

It soon became apparent that the Japanese had no intention of giving Burma real independence, and their arrogant attitude toward the Burmese fueled Burmese interest in rethinking their alignment. Secretly they began to make contact with the British and in 1944 established the Anti-Fascist People's Freedom League (AFPFL) to assist England. After the Japanese drive to invade India through Manipur failed and the British held at Imphal, the British began the slow reconquest of Burma. As they did so, the Burma government in exile at Simla in India prepared to reestablish British rule. The British were assisted by U.S. forces, the famed Merrill's Marauders, as well as by the Chinese and special British detachments such as Wingate's Raiders and Force 101, which worked with the Kachin, and Force 136, which had Karen assistance. This bloody and destructive enterprise was a sideshow to the main war in the Pacific, but it allowed the British to resume at least temporary control over their former colony. In March 1945, the Burmese formally sided with the British and assisted in the recapture of Rangoon.

By the end of the war, the Burmese economy was destroyed and the oil industry devastated. Land had gone out of production, and populations, both Indian and Burmese, were dislocated. The British, who had fought hard to regain Burma, were intent on keeping it under their control. They rescinded the reforms granted under the 1937 constitution and put Burma back under direct rule for a period. The Burmese, naturally, were upset, and agitation for independence increased. Enormous numbers of arms had been provided to a variety of groups, both Burman and minority, within the country. These groups, which constituted paramilitary forces, were to cause problems after independence. The AFPFL emerged as the key political organization, and allied to it was the paramilitary People's Volunteer Organization (PVO), composed of those who had not been absorbed into the Burma army. By 1946, PVO membership had reached 100,000.

The postwar change in the British administration in England, which brough the Labour party into power, also brought a reversal of British policy. The new British prime minister, Clement Attlee, met with a Burmese delegation led by Aung San to negotiate Burma's independence. The most important issue was that of the minority peoples. England had determined that they should be free to decide whether they wished to stay in an independent Burma, to be independent, or to remain under British rule. The Burmans arranged a meeting at Panglong in the Shan State and invited the minorities. The Karen, who had hoped for an independent nation because of their long association with the British and their joint participation against the Japanese, were observers. On February 12, 1947, a day still celebrated in Burma as Union Day, an agreement was announced that the Burman majority and the minorities would form a union. The Shan were given the right to secede from the union after ten years. The same right was given to the Kayah. The Kachin were promised a separate state, but were not given the privilege of succession, because the Kachin area included regions that had substantial Burman populations. The Karen opted to try to negotiate a separate agreement with the British and sent a delegation to London for that purpose. It was unsuccessful. In retrospect, the strong personality of Aung San and the trust he personally generated allowed the Panglong meeting to succeed. The unification of Burma under Aung San's unique leadership, however, proved to be short-lived.

In preparation for independence, elections for a constituent assembly were held in April 1947. The AFPFL, under the leadership of Aung San, won handily, capturing 248 of the 255 seats. The Karen National Union, a grouping of many Karen factions, boycotted the election. The opening ceremony on June 9 elected U Nu as president of the assembly. A constitution committee was appointed to draft the proposed basic law of the new government. During the drafting period, however, Aung San and five of his top cabinet officials were assassinated. July 19, 1947, the day the assassinations took place, is still venerated as the most solemn day in Burma, Martyr's Day. Investigation revealed that the crime was ordered by U Saw, a prewar politician who perhaps hoped to create from the chaos that might ensue a leadership role for himself in the new government. He was later tried and executed.

Drafting of the constitution of the Union of Burma, as the nation was to be called, was finally concluded. It created a new country that opted to remain outside the British Commonwealth. It was to have a bicameral legislature, with a House of Nationalities, seats allotted by region and ethnic group, and a House of Delegates, which controlled state finances and which was national in scope. The constitution was mildly socialist. Ownership of land was vested in the state, but the document, which drew upon the British parliamentary system, was democratic in spirit. The constitution, as one of its drafters indicated later, was federal in theory but unitary in practice. The treaty of independence was finally signed in London by Mr. Attlee and U Nu on October 17, 1947.

On the death of Aung San, the untried U Nu became the leader of the newly independent nation as well as the head of the coalition political party, the AFPFL. Burma became one country, but the constitution's solution to the minority problems was short-lived. As Burma entered a new era, strains quickly became apparent, and the nation was hard pressed to cope with its economic and political problems.

3

The Resurgence of Burmese Identity

Burmese political, economic, and social attitudes and aspirations since independence have been profoundly influenced by three interacting forces: nationalism, socialism, and Buddhism. Historically, nationalism and socialism were in part responses to the colonial political and economic experience and to the alienation of the population from the sources of societal control. Buddhism acquired new vigor and a more pronounced role because of its close association with both nationalism and socialism.

The colonial period spawned political and economic alienation, especially among the Burmans. Economic alienation, largely the product of another colony (India), was encouraged officially and unofficially by Britain. Socialism was a reaction to Burman economic degradation and was reinforced both by traditional elements of Burman thought, including Buddhism, and by the prevailing intellectual climate in England and in India in the 1930s. The separation of the more modern elements of the economy, and indeed many traditional economic activities, from the Burman populace strongly influenced contemporary economic and political dynamics. Political alienation was twofold: Burmans were separated by the British and Indians from the sources of effective power, while they saw the British share such power in India, and they were isolated from most of the minority groups.

ALIENATION AND THE GROWTH OF NATIONALISM

The British piecemeal partition, and eventual conquest, of all of Burma destroyed more than a traditional regime. It eliminated not only the seat of secular authority, the monarchy, but obliterated the religio-mystical functions of the head of state and all the institutions and customs that were predicated on his role. The monarchy disappeared, and with it evaporated elements of a society that slowly had to be

35

recreated and shaped to fit a new era in Burma. The palace symbolically was Mount Meru, the mystical center of the universe, and each element in the palace corresponded to some natural or physical attribute. The king ritually contributed to the fertility of the land by plowing, and he brought the rains. He was the defender of the faith, Buddhism. In the absence of a professional bureaucracy, as in the Sinocentric societies, his removal caused the collapse of the court-focused state. Dacoity and rebellions spread after his ouster. They were not only directed against a foreign invader but were in response to a political vacuum that succeeded the demise of traditional administration.

For a system based on moral (Buddhist) law, the British substituted an alien administrative machine that had two functions—maintaining law and order and collecting revenue—and in the process overturned traditional institutions from the highest level to the village. This change subverted the effectiveness of these institutions in upholding the traditional moral, economic, and political order. Alienation was thus partially a product of enforced institutional change. Many such changes were based on Indian precedents.

The British fought the Anglo-Burmese wars from India, using supplies from India and Indian troops and officers stationed in India. To those far from the Burmese scene who did not understand Burma or its history, it made sense to rule Burma through the country in the region where the British had the greatest power and the longest tradition rather than through Whitehall. The conquest of Burma was, after all, a product of an expansionist colonial policy that was India centered. It was also bureaucratically convenient. No other decision except that of annexation, however, had such a disastrous impact on Burma or contributed as much to the growth of Burmese nationalism and, indeed, to the strengthening of Burmese xenophobia.

It was also convenient to adopt, wholesale, Indian administrative models that were not relevant to Burma. They too had dire consequences. For example, the role of the headman, the elemental economic and social institution at the local level, was completely reversed to conform to an Indian model. Under the monarchy, the headman's role, with variations in Lower and in Upper Burma, was to control what today in Burma might be a township. He was either determined by heredity or chosen by a consensual, if not democratic, system. According to this system, recognized leaders appointed a village representative to the central government to protect the village's interests in dealings with lower-echelon officials, whom the king had appointed. The British retained the headman, but reduced his authority to that of a village functionary. Instead of acting as the highest official at the local level, the headman became under the British the lowest official of the central administration representing an even smaller administrative unit, the village. As a result, the role of headman atrophied. Although he continued to settle disputes informally, so as to avoid government interference with village life, he lost both his ability to serve as an efficient mechanism for autonomous local administration and growth and his role as the nexus of village life. In addition, administrative units were created. Burma Proper was divided into divisions, and the divisions into districts, the latter becoming the heart of the new administration. Western legal processes were introduced as well.

Institutions changed, but just as profound a transformation was wrought by the large influx of foreigners into Burma, mainly from India. The presence of foreigners was nothing new in Burma, but their numbers and powers were of a substantially different magnitude. The upper and middle echelons of the colonial administration were staffed by the British from the Indian Civil Service, and their presence extended in the countryside to the district level. The British also ran a large part of the burgeoning private trade, both domestic and foreign, such obvious government functions as the army and police, and a variety of services established throughout Burma. They were a minority of the official community, however, and an even smaller minority outside the capital; for it was essential, if Burma was to pay for itself, that lower-salaried functionaries form the bulk of the bureaucracy. These functionaries could be found in India before they could be recruited and trained in Burma.

On the arrival of the British, Burma was a series of village communities radiating from a small number of towns. As the British began to build the infrastructure to make the economy pay for itself—the bureaucracy, the railroads, surplus rice production and exportation, a teak industry, and the administration of ports—both skilled and unskilled labor was required and, at the higher levels, labor with a knowledge of English.

Under these circumstances, where else but to India would the British turn for such labor? There had grown up in India generations of professionals and paraprofessionals and a wide range of others with equally needed skills who knew and could work with the British. In 1917, the secretary of state for India announced in Parliament that it was government policy to place as many Indians as possible in the Burmese administration. In addition, the demand for manual labor increased as Rangoon and other cities grew.

Indian immigration into Burma was sizable and encouraged. Indeed, it was sometimes subsidized by lowering ship passage rates from India. Much of the influx of this labor was seasonal. It continued to grow, although the ebb and flow of sea traffic between India and Rangoon took back a large number every year. Between 1913 and 1929, over 4.5 million Indians entered Rangoon, whereas less than 3.5 million returned to India during the same period. The residue, 1.1 million, remained. Perhaps 60 percent of the annual immigrants resided in Rangoon, which became an Indian city. In 1901, it was 48 percent Indian. In 1931, it was 53 percent; the Burmese numbered 32 percent. Rangoon's Indian population was evident in the mosques and Hindu temples that dotted the downtown area, and the Indian administrative influence was manifest in the monumental colonial architecture of red and cream stone – a visual reminder that Rangoon was indeed governed from Calcutta.

Complex social and economic problems resulted. Migration was overwhelmingly male, which inevitably led to social problems. Indebtedness was widespread. A type of indentured servitude existed under which the laborer arrived in Rangoon under contract, already in debt from the ship passage and having no recourse out of the spiral of increased debt and partial repayment but more work. Under the *maistry*, or "contractor," system, the contractor recruited, shipped, and paid the laborers at the behest of some industrial plant. Few local loyalties were possible in such circumstances. Certain occupations, such as the port and shipping fields, became Indian preserves. In Rangoon, the center of Burmese industry, Indians held 62 percent of all skilled positions and about 95 percent of unskilled jobs. In the Irrawaddy Delta in 1931, Indians held 65.8 percent of trade positions, 52.1 percent of public administration jobs, 36.3 percent of jobs in transport, and the same percentage in industry. There was no possibility for the Burmans to adjust to these new economic conditions or to acquire entrepreneurial talents. The labor vacuum was already filled at all levels by Indians, and it would take a world war and then a revolution to loosen the grip of the Indian community on much of the economic life of Burma.

With the advent of steam navigation, commerce, no longer curtailed by the seasonal monsoons, prospered. Even before the opening of the Suez Canal in 1869 made European markets more accessible, Burma was exporting 400,000 tons of rice to India. Indian merchants, petty traders, and the Chettyars (Indian moneylenders) began to find their way to Burma to take advantage of the new economic growth. Agricultural credit and related trade and marketing were essential in order to open the vast and potentially rich lands of the Irrawaddy Delta after the Second Anglo-Burmese War (1852), and the Indians supplied them. As the Burmans began to migrate south to partake of the expanded opportunities for the new, developing monoculture, Indians also began to move into the farm areas to work as seasonal landless laborers, needed for planting and harvesting. As the Burmans contracted greater debts, which they had difficulty repaying under an economic and legal system they did not fully appreciate, the Indians—working at appreciably lower rates—became tenants on much of the rice land.

Thus, as their country was beginning to go through the birth pangs of economic growth, Burmans were effectively excluded from most aspects of that growth. They continued to be farmers, especially on marginal land; a few were in the traditional extractive industries (those held as monopolies by the monarch); some remained petty traders in the bazaars.

The need for trade also brought in the Chinese, who had been in Burma from traditional times, but in smaller numbers. They were more easily assimilated because of physical similarity and religious affinity, even though the Chinese (Mahayanists) and the Burmans (Theravada Buddhists) adhered to different schools of Buddhism. As time passed, the Anglo-Burmans and Anglo-Indians, who numbered about 25,000 before World War II, also commanded certain occupations. Thus, until late in the colonial period, the Burmans were cut out of the rewards, but not the dire effects, of the political and economic changes that had begun to have such an impact in the country.

The prewar figures on employment demonstrate this alienation. The Burmans in 1931 were 65.7 percent of the population; "other indigenous groups" were 24.6 percent, whereas the Indians numbered 7 percent and the Chinese 1.3 percent. Indians born outside of Burma were 7.9 percent of the labor force, but they were employed in 36.3 percent of all mining jobs, 14.7 percent of industry, 43.2 percent of transport, 15.6 percent of trade, 43.3 percent of the public forces, and 26.6 percent of public administration positions. The Chinese, at 1.5 percent of the labor force, held 9.7 percent of the mining and 6.9 percent of trade jobs.

Major centers of growth were dominated by foreigners. Other towns beside Rangoon had substantial foreign populations. Pegu in 1931 was 25.1 percent Indian, and Toungoo 26 percent. In 1930, 82.8 percent of bankers and moneylenders in Rangoon, and 51.4 percent of that group in district towns, was Indian. There were no Burmese listed in this occupation in Rangoon, and only 34.3 percent of those in the districts was Burmese.

There was an ethnic division of labor. The Burmans were on the lower rungs of the economic ladder, in agriculture at the mercy of foreign moneylenders at home and the world market price for rice abroad. Few could have middle-class aspirations, and the middle class, until well after independence, was essentially Indian and Chinese. In addition, the Burmans were ill-adapted to deal with the widespread, rapid economic changes within Burma Proper. Traditionally, they had accumulated wealth not for economic investment, but for religious or psychic reward – a better life to ensure a higher future incarnation and enhanced social esteem – and for sheer ostentation. They were not entrepreneurs, for there was no possibility of private economic expansion under a system in which the monarchy dominated all lucrative economic functions.

The situation was tolerable only because the Burmans, although pauperized, were not starving. With the advent of the great depression and the resultant fall in the world price for rice, the situation deteriorated. The Burmese price for paddy declined from 200 rupees per 100 baskets of 46 pounds each in 1928 to R120 in 1929, R80 in 1930, and R60 in 1931, which was below the cost of production. An official British report noted that the price of paddy was "lower than anything in the memory of living man." Living standards fell; land was foreclosed. Chettyar firms, with a combined capital of $300 million in 1929, controlled most of the best agricultural land as a result. Their holdings grew from 6 percent in 1930 to 25 percent in 1936, as debts went unpaid, and land – the security for loans – passed to them. They held 2.5 million out of 10 million acres of the leading Lower Burma rice-producing areas. The Chettyars also held mortgages on an additional 10 to 20 percent of the land. It is unlikely that more than 15 percent of Lower Burma land in 1941 was owned by farmers and was unmortgaged.

The Burmans became prey to increased discontent, which took the form of heightened dacoity, producing one of the highest per capita crime rates in the world. In 1930, the Saya San Rebellion erupted and became most widespread where tenancy and land alienation were very high. The rebellion had its origins in mystical and magical forms of traditional Burmese religious and royal beliefs, but the economic degradation, so prevalent in parts of Burma, contributed to its spread.

For a long period, the Burmese were also excluded from the higher levels of the bureaucracy. It was only in 1923 that a Burmese passed the Indian Civil Service examinations, although four had previously been appointed. Burmese representation at professional levels continued to be small until the close of the colonial era. The Burma army reflected the skewing of staffing, in this case of the Burmans. In 1940, only 12 percent of the army was Burman. Karen, Kachin, and Chin levies formed the nucleus of the indigenous forces.

Discrimination, coupled with economic depression, began to produce unrest that was directed toward the foreign community. Discontent centered not only on the colonial masters, but on the Indians, who were associated with the British. The 1930 Rangoon dock strike, which pitted Burmese against Indians, resulted in riots in which about 100 people were killed and 1,000 injured. Serious violence again erupted in 1938 against the Indian Muslims as a result of some inflammatory literature published by the Muslims. Whatever the immediate spark, the long pent-up economic and social frustration against the Indians was apparent in the riots that followed. Buddhist nationalism had grown, and monks were directly involved in those riots.

THE ORIGINS OF SOCIALISM IN BURMA

Contemporary socialist ideas entered Burma late relative to other Asian societies. This was due in part to an enforced intellectual isolation of Burma from modern trends. To prevent ferment, the British had at first been reluctant to introduce institutions of higher learning, and when they did, contemporary events were not taught. There were even problems concerning the registration of the scholarly Burma Research Society (1910) until it agreed to eschew study of the contemporary period. This enforced isolation extended to the exclusion of some international organizations. Although international Communist activity pervaded much of Asia in the 1920s, and Burma may have come under the jurisdiction of the Comintern's Shanghai Bureau, there is no evidence that Comintern workers carried out any activities in Burma during that period. The influence of the Indian Congress party and its anticolonial activities was of greater significance within Burma.

The first Communist materials to enter Burma were brought back by a Burmese state scholar who had met a Burmese member of the British Communist party in England. Ironically, the spread of socialist thought came from the royalties of a book by the arch royalist and pretender to the peacock throne, Saya San, who was executed as a rebel. These funds were used to establish a small library of books, including *Das Kapital*, portions of which U Nu later translated. These works circulated widely among the small intellectual elite involved in the nationalist movement. Such books had great influence only among a select few, but their ideas spread as they were articulated by the leadership at mass meetings.

The introduction of socialist thought in Burma in the 1930s was also fostered by two brothers who studied in Europe and later assumed positions of importance. They were U Ba Han and U Ba Maw. Dr. Ba Maw, later prime minister, founded the Sinyetha ("Poor Man's party"), which introduced the "rudimentary principles of socialism" to the Burmese. Dr. Ba Han was influential in spreading socialist thought at the University of Rangoon, where he was a member of the law faculty and legal adviser to the student union. Close to Ba Han was U Ba Nyein, an ardent socialist who later assumed a role of great importance as civilian economic adviser to General Ne Win following the military coup of 1962.

The anticapitalist and pro-Marxist volume *The Capitalist World,*

published in 1939 by U Ba Hein, was another influence on socialist economic thought in Burma. Leftist study groups were formed by such eminent individuals as Thakin Kodaw Hmaing. Aung San and Ne Win both
participated in these groups. Thirteen of the many Burmese leaders who
in 1931 called themselves *thakin* ("lord," or "master") formed a study
group in 1938 that was the first Communist cell in Burma as well as the
initial core of the Communist party of Burma. (*Thakin,* a term similar to
sahib in India, was usually reserved for the British but the Burmese used
it, perhaps with sarcasm, to demonstrate their equality.)

Socialism spread rapidly among the elite. In 1936, J. S. Furnivall, a
retired British civil servant, Burmese nationalist, and later author of two
seminal books on Burma, founded Burma's Fabian League. In 1937, U
Nu, later to be prime minister, formed the Nagani ("Red Dragon") Book
Club to foster left-wing thought. The Nagani had 217 members and
modeled itself on Victor Gallanz's Left Book Club in London. They
issued seventy books before the war. By 1939, U Ba Swe and U Kyaw
Nyein, both socialists and future political leaders, had formed a secret
organization, the Burma Revolutionary party, which was later to become
the nucleus of the future socialist party. The same year, the first successful workers and peasants' union was formed. The most important
contribution of Marxism and the Left to Burma's nationalist efforts, however, was not in ideology or in garnering international recognition;
rather, it was in the concept of mobilizing indigenous mass support. This
concept was new to the Burmese nationalist movement and contrasted
sharply with previous strikes and Buddhist expressions of ferment,
which were either elite or worker oriented.

BUDDHISM AND NATIONALISM

Burmese intellectuals were skeptical of foreign contacts and
developed their own approach to social issues, one centered on
socialism. There were inextricable ties in Burma that eventually linked
nationalism, socialism, and Buddhism. Burman identification of nationhood with Buddhism was clear and persistent. Most politicians, including the most modern, have associated themselves with the revival of
Buddhism.

The links between Buddhism and nationalism were forged on the
British annexation of Upper Burma. British policy was to eliminate the
thathanabaing (the "supreme patriarch") of the loosely structured Buddhist hierarchy in Burma. The destruction of the king's role as the
defender of the faith and the removal of the *thathanabaing* disestablished
Buddhism. The Burmans had a real fear that the Christian invaders were

destroying their religion. Christian missionaries were prevalent in Burma, and not only among the hill tribes. Secular education made inroads on a field traditionally reserved for the *sangha*. Since public expression of nationalist sentiments through the formation of political organizations was outlawed by the secular colonial state, it was natural that these feelings and their organizational expression were first articulated through Buddhist groups, such as the Young Men's Buddhist Association (YMBA), founded in 1906 on the Christian model, and the General Council of Burmese (Buddhist) Organizations started in 1922. By 1916, the YMBA had begun publicly to express concern over British religious policy.

Buddhism was not only central to the Burman personality, it became, within bounds, a sanctioned form of nationalistic expression as well. Reverence for the sanctity of the pagodas was hardly a political offense, even though it served a political purpose. However, this nationalism was more fervently expressed by some Buddhist monks and, according to the British, amounted to sedition. The most famous of the nationalist monks was U Ottama. In 1921, he returned from India strongly influenced by Gandhi's nonviolent resistance movement. He advocated independence and was arrested in 1921. The following year he was released, but spent the years 1924–1927 and 1928–1929 in jail for anti-British activities, after which he died. Another of the Buddhist monk-martyrs to the nationalist cause was U Wisara, who died in a Rangoon jail in 1929 after a hunger strike. Monks were also involved in, and sometimes led, the anti-Indian riots of the 1930s. The Shwedagon Pagoda grounds and hill were used for some of the anti-British student protests of the same period, and the area continues to be a site for demonstrations. British insistence on wearing shoes, traditionally removed in any Burmese home, at Buddhist pagodas effectively excluded the casual colonial visitor from this realm, although it did not deter the troops. (Wearing shoes before Burmese monarchs had earlier been a symbolic point of contention between the two cultures.) The hill on which the pagoda sits visually commands the area, preventing surprise attacks on those occupying the site. The solace and legitimacy that occupation of such a sacred place gave, however, were more significant. The Shwedagon in Rangoon is, as Proust wrote of the church at Combray, "the church epitomizing the town, representing it, speaking of it and for it to the horizon." Thus, gravitation toward the Shwedagon was both symbolic and real. It took political and social issues and brought them together under the physical symbol of the primordial Burman loyalty, the most sacred Buddhist pagoda. In 1974, when students demonstrated over the proper burial site for U Thant, these disturbances naturally centered on the Shwedagon.

The dynamic interplay of Buddhism, socialism, and nationalism in the Burmese context has been continuous since the 1930s. At that time, socialist thought began to permeate Burmese intellectual circles, and intellectuals began to reexamine Buddhism in the light of these new secular ideas. This inquiry had begun much earlier, soon after the turn of the century in India, Ceylon, and Japan. In Burma, there was an interpretation, or reinterpretation, of the Ashokan Buddhist political and economic ideal—a Buddhist welfare state—and an equating of that ideal with contemporary Burmese nationalist and social needs. Whether such an interpretation was doctrinally correct is of less importance than the fact that Buddhism appeared crucial to the amalgamation of nationalist ideas with a new economic system that would better the lot of the Burmans, avoid the economic disintegration of the Burman majority, which was everywhere evident, and justify the modern economic functions of a state that would eliminate exploitation. Basically, the function of the state, as it was conceived, was to establish economic conditions for the populace that would allow them an opportunity for meditation and thus eventual salvation.

The natural interplay between the Buddhist resurgence and nationalism was heightened by the use of Buddhist terminology to express the new socialist concepts. Many of the abstract terms of the Burmese language had their origins in ancient Pali, the language of the Burmese Buddhist scriptures. Socialism was introduced to the masses in these terms. Buddhist and Marxist concepts were equated. The Buddhist principle of causality was equivalent to Marxist dialectics, and liberation from impermanence was equated with social liberation through revolutionary struggle. The term for a labor strike was synonymous with the Buddhist term for a monk overturning his begging bowl, thus not allowing the people to gain merit by making offerings of food. This was a most serious act. There was both a congruence of terms and people. Thakin Soe, later founder of the Red Flag (Trotskyite) Communist movement, had studied Buddhism and later translated some socialist literature into Burmese, as did U Nu. U Nu later used Buddhist expressions to describe to the masses the welfare state for which he labored. He compared it to the *padaythabin*, or the tree of fulfillment in Buddhist legend.

The equating of capitalism and Christianity under the British demonstrated to many during this period—including key figures such as U Nu—that capitalism had turned people away from Buddhism, that it encouraged greed, and that its elimination would be a good Buddhist deed. The interplay between Buddhism and socialism in that period was so complete that there was even an association of Marxist monks within the Buddhist *sangha*.

STUDENT NATIONALISM

As early as 1894, less than a decade after the conquest of Upper Burma and during the pacification of some of the remoter regions, a new elite channel was founded. That year, University College, a branch of the University of Calcutta, was formed in Rangoon. It was followed by the founding of Judson College, a Baptist institution named after the most famous of the missionaries to Burma. By 1920, plans were made to form a new university in Burma on the Oxford-Cambridge model, combining the two colleges. To be called Rangoon University, it was designed as an elite institution with selective entry and high standards. The formation of the university was the cause of the first of many student strikes, because the students, whose agitation spread to other cities besides Rangoon, wanted a more egalitarian institution that would broaden the base of the new emerging Burmese leadership.

The strike eventually died out, but not before the students had established their nationalistic credentials to the public. Also, occupying the Shwedagon Pagoda grounds during the strike lent their secular leadership role a form of spiritual authority. The student strike is thus regarded a singularly important event in the history of Burmese nationalism even today.

Student discontent over the next fifteen years was superseded by more widespread unrest. The Saya San Rebellion and workers' strikes were responses in part to the deteriorating economic conditions exacerbated by the depression. However, students outside of the campus became part of the new nationalist elite. They formed the Dobama Asiayone ("We Burmans Association") and called themselves *thakin* in 1931 in defiance of custom, which reserved the term for the British. Thus, they demonstrated their equality with the colonialists. Most of the leaders in Burma in the early years following independence were involved in the Thakin movement.

It was in 1936, however, that those who would eventually lead Burma to independence gained prominence. A student strike that year involved U Nu, Aung San, and Kyaw Nyein, among others, and resulted from a confrontation between the university authorities and the student union over the activities of a faculty member. Although initially of no political importance, the strike became the focus of anti-British sentiment and spread to high schools throughout the country. It eventually led to a reorganization of the university system, but more importantly it enhanced the stature of both the participants and the nationalist movement, while increasing the authority of the student union. Student strikes occurred again in 1938, and during that year students picketed the government secretariat. The police opened fire and killed one student, resulting in a major government inquiry into the incident. Strikes also took place in 1939 at Mandalay Intermediate College and in other cities.

The results of these strikes for the nationalists were more important, however, than the causes. A new generation of leaders trained themselves through political agitation at the University of Rangoon. They regarded themselves, and in turn were regarded, as the leaders of the nationalist movement. They organized student unions, addressed crowds, wrote tracts, and read literature that supported their aspirations for independence, with which Buddhism and socialism became closely associated. They also were influenced by the Indian independence and Irish nationalist movements, as well as by fascist thought.

World War II gave a new sense of urgency and opportunity to these student leaders. Some, such as Aung San, became one of the Thirty Comrades, who were trained by the Japanese. Others remained in Burma and helped organize the Japanese-endorsed Burma branch of the East Asiatic Youth League. Following the Allied victory, the student cadre of the 1930s was transformed into the new national leadership that had to negotiate for and plan a new independent state.

THE FRAGILITY OF THE UNION— ETHNICITY AND IDENTITY

The growth of antiforeign nationalism had its effect upon the relations among internal ethnic groups, groups that had had little formal interaction since the British conquest. Anti-Indian attitudes proved persistent, but internal ethnic antagonism was to influence Burma's future more. For the past three decades of independent rule, the history of Burma seems a maze of insurgencies and rebellions. Some were politically motivated, but more were products of ethnic discontent. The ebb and flow of these insurgencies are confusing even to experienced observers of the Burmese scene.

In the light of Burma's present problems of ethnicity, it is not surprising to find Burmese history written as a form of ethnic struggle: the Burman conquest of the Mon capital of Thaton in the eleventh century, the Shan domination of central Burma following the Mongol conquest in 1287, resurgent Mon kingdoms in the south finally subdued by the Burmans in the eighteenth century, the Burman expeditions against the Arakanese and the final incorporation of these people into the Burmese state in 1784.

Nevertheless, the temptation to weave the present and the past into a single analytic pattern, relating the growth of contemporary ethnic insurgency to traditional struggles for control over such groups, should be resisted. It oversimplifies the historical evidence, counting ethnicity as the primary or sole factor in monarchical power struggles. At the same time, it discounts the fundamental discontinuity in the interrelations of ethnic groups between the traditional period and the present. The hiatus in political interaction between the Burmans and the minorities during the British administration is important to an understanding of the present.

Of all the problems facing Burma, none appeared as intractable as the issue of the "union" of Burma – the fusion of different ethnic peoples into a nation with a set of overarching common goals and aspirations. The term connotes an ideal polity, but the reality is quite different.

Ethnicity in the Burmese context should now be understood as a series of highly complex, evolving relationships that vary among and between ethnic peoples and are ever in a state of flux. Historically, these relationships were never stable with a single established pattern of response. In part, relations were dependent upon the particular groups interacting, their economic and political relations, the resources (military, economic, strategic) at their command, and their distance from the centers of political and military influence. Ethnicity did not guarantee a predetermined response to change. A Kachin under certain circumstances might act as a Shan, or a Mon as a Burman. Wars that were commonly regarded as ethnic may have had their origins in such economic causes as control over areas of surplus rice production and their populations or over highly strategic trade routes. Since distances were great, administrative capacity limited, and manpower requirements heavy, direct rule over peoples of marginal importance to the center was inappropriate as long as suzerainty was acknowledged.

Colonial rule changed this situation. The Burman monarch, who in general controlled all minorities loosely, was replaced by a new power – Britain – which commanded obeisance from all groups, Burmans and minorities alike. Colonial rule increased the center's control over minorities. Perceiving the need to define borders, create revenue, pacify tribes, and bring Christianity to the heathen, the British pushed administration to the political frontiers. In so doing, they broke the traditional patterns of accommodation that existed among the groups of Burma, substituting a system under which all indigenous peoples reported, so to speak, to a foreigner.

The administration of colonial Burma reinforced this new pattern. Burma Proper, encompassing those areas where the Burmans (including, at that time, the Arakanese and the Mon) were in the majority, was administered as one unit. Late in the colonial period, Burma Proper was given a modicum of self-government, whereas the hill regions of Burma were the "scheduled areas," outside of normal adminstrative patterns and under varying degrees of direct British control. Each area of Burma had its special history. The Kayah State was never conquered by the British, and the Burman monarch recognized its independence in 1875. The Chin Hills were not incorporated into Burma until ten years after the annexation of the Mandalay kingdom. The Shan states each differed and had varying degrees of local autonomy, and their *sawbwa*s retained a degree of authority.

If the traditional ethnic relationships no longer had meaning after the colonial conquest, no new relationships had developed by World War II. The war not only brought about the destruction of the economy, but also broke the pattern of forced minority isolation. As British administrative power disintegrated in the face of Japanese expansion, new tensions developed that were in part a product of the past and in part a result of the war and the Japanese promises of independence to Burma. Thus, the Burmans initially fought alongside the Japanese, while the Karen and Kachin sided with the British. The first major instances of communal disintegration among indigenous ethnic groups were the Burman-Karen riots in the delta and the Salween District in 1942, at the time the British were withdrawing and before the Japanese had fully occupied the areas. They were the harbinger of worse clashes years later. The Shan situation was somewhat different. Japan ceded Kengtung, the largest and the most autonomous of the Shan states, and Mongpan, another smaller state, to Thailand for its support in the struggle for the Greater East Asia Co-Prosperity Sphere.

The British had long used Karen troops, first to help pacify Upper Burma following the annexation and later to help put down the Saya San Rebellion. In addition to recruiting some Kachin and Chin to help in the war against Japan, the British also recruited some 12,000 Karen to carry out guerrilla activities behind Japanese lines in conjunction with British Force 136, a special detachment. The heritage of World War II was not only the rise of Burmese nationalism, but a growth of ethnic nationalism and a belief among the Karen that the British would reward them for their loyalty. As early as 1928, some Karen leaders had argued for an independent Karen state. The war reinforced these goals. The stage was set for the interplay among ethnic groups in the postwar period and for the negotiations that would lead to independence. Of all the issues facing both the British and the Burmese, and of those among the Burmese themselves, the minority problem was the most difficult. Through the personal magnetism and trust generated by General Aung San, a solution was found to this problem, a solution that unfortunately proved to be temporary.

Photographs

Kachin State – Morning Landscape.

Chin Hills – Girl Spinning (left).

Chin Hills – Haka Chin Family (below).

Kayah State – Padaung Women.

Northern Shan State –
Palaung Women.

Shan State – Lisu Child (right).

Shan State – Lisu Women
in Formal Dress.

Pagan – Ananda Temple, Begun in A.D. 1091. (Viewed from the Sulamani Temple.)

Pagan – Thatbinnyu Temple, from the Middle Twelfth Century.

54

Pagan – Thandawgya Image, from A.D. 1284.

Ava—Ruins of a Pagoda Built in the Seventeenth or Eighteenth Century.

Sagaing—In the Ruins of a Nineteenth-Century Pagoda.

Rangoon – Shwedagon Pagoda Platform During the Festival of Lights.

Rangoon – Water Festival Float with Girl Dressed as Dancer.

Lower Burma – Boy on a Water Buffalo.

Shan State – Transporting Rice on Inle Lake.

Shan State – Buddhist Monastery.

4

Independence and Civilian Rule, 1948–1962

At 4:20 on the morning of January 4, 1948, a time an astrologer chose for its auspiciousness, Burma once again became independent. It was the fourth time in Burmese history that the nation was united under an independent government. With the 1947 assassination of General Aung San, thirty-two year old architect of the new Burmese sovereignty, leadership fell on U Nu, the young and as yet untried head of the major political coalition, the Anti-Fascist People's Freedom League (AFPFL). Emerging from the last months of World War II as an amalgamation of anti-Japanese, pro-independence, military, and political forces, the AFPFL had captured the support of the full spectrum of Burmese political life except for the extreme Left and a few older politicians on the Right. The unity of the AFPFL was, however, ephemeral once its immediate goal – independence – had been achieved.

If the hour was auspicious, other auguries were not. The new government inherited a war-devastated economy, and its only immediate advantages were its surplus, but vastly reduced, food production and the enthusiasm of freedom. The Red Flag Communists were already in revolt, indicating that the left wing would make additional demands on the new state. Muslim separatists (Mujahids) were in rebellion in the Arakan, and the Karen, who had not participated formally in the Panglong Agreement, were restive. The People's Volunteer Organization (PVO), formerly under the command of General Aung San, was armed but leaderless. Its loyalties were in doubt. These signs presaged future problems. In addition, the government had a highly trained, but narrow, elite with which to govern. It had lost its cadre of experienced, expatriate civil servants. As many Indians moved back into Burma, economic power slowly accumulated in their hands once again.

Even the army was a heterogeneous collection of ethnic minorities whose loyalties were as yet untested. Its cohesiveness was further weakened by three distinct traditions: those of the British trained forces, the Japanese-sponsored troops, and the anti-Japanese guerrillas supplied by the British or Americans (Force 136 composed of Karen, Force 101 of Kachin). In 1940, the Burma army was only 12.3 percent Burman, but 27.8 percent Karen, 22.9 percent Kachin, and 22.6 percent Chin. The pro-Japanese, anti-British forces, led by Aung San, were known first as the Burma Independence Army, but were reorganized first into the Burma Defense Army by the Japanese, and later the Burma National Army. In 1947, the amalgamated Burma army was composed of fifteen regular battalions and fifteen military police battalions, a very small force with which to deal with the problems that developed.

The Union of Burma had come into existence without armed struggle through a change in British governments and through the acumen of Aung San. Neither foreign nor tried indigenous advisers were on hand to help. The new government would have to face a most uncertain future, however auspicious the date and time of its inception may have been.

THE UNION AT BAY

Within eighteen months of independence, it seemed that the laboriously constructed multiethnic Union of Burma was ready to collapse. By then the nation had exploded into a confusing series of rebellions with fluid fronts that defied demarcation. The country had to communicate by air. Land routes were often cut, and rail lines were littered with twisted freight cars testifying to the violence.

Having defected from the AFPFL in 1946, the Red Flag Communists (Trotskyite) went underground in January 1947 before independence, claiming that the new freedom from Britain was not real. The larger White Flag Communists (Burma Communist party), with the capacity to muster some 25,000 supporters and led by the able Thakin Than Tun, followed soon after independence. They fomented a series of workers' strikes that culminated on March 27, 1948, in rebellion. There is still debate as to whether their revolt, which continues, was autonomous or whether it was in response to Comintern directives that emanated from a February 1948 meeting in Calcutta of the youth groups associated with the Communist-dominated World Federation of Trade Unions. The White Flags quickly succeeded in controlling the upper Sittang valley, thus breaching the main road and the only rail line between Rangoon and Mandalay.

More complex than relations with the Communists were those with the PVO. Leaderless after the death of Aung San, but armed and with political influence inside the AFPFL, they had to be treated gingerly. The PVO itself was divided into White Band and Yellow Band factions, the former the larger group and Communist oriented, the latter more moderate. Government relations with the PVO depended upon delicate negotiations concerning how far left the Union was prepared to go. These internal deliberations centered on the forging of a party platform that came to be known as the Leftist Unity Program. Finally approved on July 2, 1948, it contained the seeds of the socialist programs of all future governments, including provisions on land reform, lowering of rents, state ownership of the export trade, and the formation of people's councils at the village level. The most controversial provision was the establishment under government auspices, and presumably with government funds, of a Marxist league that would spread the Marxist doctrine. Delicate negotiations finally eliminated that element of the plan, but the result was the resignation of the cabinet and the revolution of the White Band PVO on July 29, 1948. This disaster was followed in August by the mutiny of two of the five battalions of the Burma Rifles. While the White Flag Communists held critical areas of the Sittang valley, the White Band PVO held large sections of the Irrawaddy valley from the delta to Prome, about 150 miles north of Rangoon.

The rebellions culminated with that of the Karen. Long disturbed over the prospects of Burman domination, and with the memory of the Burman massacres of Karen in the delta and the Salween District in the early days of World War II, they had formed the Karen National Defense Organization (KNDO) to protect their interests. In July 1947, before independence, they occupied Moulmein, withdrawing only after reaching agreement with the Burma army that they could defend their critical areas.

Many of the Karen, split among themselves, were dissatisfied with the constitutional provisions calling for a small, isolated special Karen region called Kawthulay. Instead, some wanted a Karen-Mon state encompassing the Tenasserim Division. Other Karen desired inclusion of a large part of Lower Burma (excluding Rangoon) in such a state, as the Karen were scattered through the region. In no locale did they constitute a majority, however. The price of Karen quiescence at independence was the provision of the command of the Burma army to General Smith Dun, a Karen, who represented the largest component of the Burma army. Many other key positions within the army were also held by Karen. Karen resistance began in September 1948 and spread through the Mon areas and to the Kayah State (known as Karenni, literally "red Karen," a designation derived from dress not political coloration). A Burman massacre of Karen in Mergui District on Christmas Eve 1948 further inflamed feelings.

The Karen rebellion broke out formally in January 1949 in Bassein in the Irrawaddy Delta, Toungoo in the Sittang valley, and in Insein, on the outskirts of Rangoon. Most of the Karen regiments in the army revolted. Pa-O groups in the southern Shan State — linguistic relatives of the Karen — joined them. U Nu forced the retirement of General Smith Dun, although he remained loyal to the government. His deputy, General Ne Win, took command, a leadership role that he has held ever since in one form or another. The Karen took a number of major cities, which they held for short periods, and only the loyalty of the Chin army regulars, who were thereafter called in to control major disturbances in Rangoon, saved the capital.

The tide of rebellions swirled throughout Burma. Mandalay fell on March 13 to the KNDO and Communists, Taunggyi to the Karen on August 13. In all, thirty-one major cities and towns were held for various periods by the Karen, Communists, PVO, and Mujahids. Slowly, however, their momentum began to wane as the government reestablished military control over the major urban areas, if not a good part of the countryside. A two-pronged attack on Rangoon, one from Prome and another from Toungoo, was defeated. The state survived. Its survival could be attributed to the inability of the various insurrections, each with separate political or ethnic objectives, to coordinate their offensives or agree among themselves on their timing or plans, as well as to the loyalty of the rest of the Burma army. The leadership of U Nu was also vitally important at this critical time. The government, with its headquarters in Rangoon and access to the outside world, had a distinct advantage, although few nations provided material support. Some in the West felt that Burma was moving toward the Communist bloc and therefore morally, if not materially, supported the Karen, who were staunchly anti-Communist. There are allegations that some former British members of Force 136 assisted the Karen.

These internal rebellions were further complicated in 1952 by the expansion of the Kuomintang (KMT, or Chinese Nationalist) forces. They had retreated from China from 1948 to 1950 and crossed into the Shan State to escape from the Chinese Communist forces, much as the last Ming dynasty pretender did in 1656 when the Manchu Ch'ing dynasty took over Yunnan. These forces battled with the Burma army in 1950. China had long had interests in that region, for Chinese Nationalist forces had occupied a good part of that area in 1944 as the Japanese were retreating. The Chinese established control over broad areas and were supplied from Taiwan with U.S. connivance. The KMT invasion was accompanied by the expulsion of local Burmese officials, and KMT efforts to attract support from other dissidents reached its peak in 1952–1953, diverting government troops needed to contain the other rebellions. Burma, always concerned over the need to deal carefully with China, and under pressure from the left wing of the AFPFL, cut off U.S. assistance.

Although these rebellions receded, they did not disappear. Indeed, the Karen still fight along the eastern frontier, if not in the Rangoon suburbs. The White Flags, now known as the Burma Communist party, continue their insurrection centered along the China border in the Shan State, with outlying elements active in the Arakan and Tenasserim regions. Some of the KMT troops were evacuated; others found refuge in northwest Thailand on the border with Burma, whereas still others remain in the Shan State. The Red Flag rebellion collapsed in 1970 with the capture of Thakin Soe, and the People's Volunteer Organization was eliminated. No longer fragile, the Union of Burma is still far from united.

PARTY POLITICS IN CIVILIAN BURMA

U Nu and his government weathered the early period of the insurrections, but they had yet to build a nation and establish its credibility internally and to the outside world. In line with the regime's socialist premises, which included not only state ownership of industry but greater public access to social services, the government made efforts to expand health services and education. Soon after independence, Burma nationalized key British firms, such as the Irrawaddy Flotilla Company. The process of Burmanization of the economy had begun. It included not only nationalization, but land reform, for much of the agricultural land was still legally in the hands of the Indians. The Chettyars were not allowed to return to Burma, but the process of redistribution of land was slow, and compensation miniscule.

Internally, U Nu was concerned about the welfare of the population. He established industries, such as the Burma Pharmaceutical Company to manufacture vitamin tablets, but he thought of it more as a welfare program, part of the Pyidawtha ("Happy Land") welfare state, than as an economically self-sufficient enterprise. He distributed books in Burmese through the Burma Translation Society, which he created, and it devised programs for the newly literate. This plan harked back to a similar one that Dr. Ba Maw had initiated under the Japanese. U Nu convened the Sixth Great Buddhist Synod in 1953, ostensibly to clarify and correct the Buddhist scriptures, but also to provide legitimacy and focus for the regime. He founded the Buddha Sasana Council to print the Buddhist texts, and upon completion of the synod, formed the International Institute for Advanced Buddhistic Studies. He built the World Peace Pagoda, much as the Burmese monarchs built pagodas at Pagan.

Externally, Burma fostered socialism. It cosponsored and provided the secretariat for the Asian Socialist Conference in 1953 and the Colombo Plan conference in 1954. After an early and unsuccessful effort to interest the United States in forming a Pacific defense pact, Burma turned neutralist and was active at the Bandung meeting in Indonesia in 1955, which led to the nonaligned movement, and tried to maintain good relations with all powers.

The AFPFL, born of the struggle against Japan and sustained by the drive for independence, was by its nature an amalgam of forces held together by the overriding importance of its primary objective – independence. Once that objective had been achieved, centrifugal forces and personal ambition were bound to cause dissension. Founded in 1944, the AFPFL was an alliance that included a wide range of political views, from mildly socialist to Communist. Until 1950, the Burma Workers and Peasants' party, the aboveground arm of the White Flag Communists, was aligned with the AFPFL, as was earlier the White Band PVO. Under the umbrella AFPFL (as under the Burma Socialist Programme party in the 1960s and 1970s), a variety of mass and class organizations provided support to the parent organization, as well as the sources of personal loyalty for some of its leadership. These included the All-Burma Peasants' Organization (led by Thakin Tin), the Trades Union Congress of Burma, the Federation of Trades Organizations, and other more specialized groupings. These entities enabled their leadership to negotiate for critical ministerial positions and provided a great deal of social mobility. The resulting rivalry and dissension were major causes of the eventual demise of the AFPFL.

In its first democratic period following independence and prior to the military caretaker government of 1958, the government held two elections, in 1951 and 1956. Both were won by U Nu, as leader of the AFPFL. The first election, postponed because of the insurrections, began in June 1951 and was spaced over some months because of security problems. The AFPFL won an overwhelming victory against its two major opposition parties, the Burma Workers and Peasants' party on the Left, which won twelve seats, and the centrist party of elder politicians from the prewar period. An Arakanese opposition party, also on the Right, won several seats from that region. In effect, the AFPFL, by virtue of its broad base if not its coherent ideology, governed in that period under single-party rule. It was democratic, however, and concessions continuously had to be made to the Left.

Because of deteriorating economic conditions following the drop in the world price of rice after the Korean War, the AFPFL did less well in the 1956 elections. Their margin of victory was 186 seats to 68 for the opposition. The rise in the number (48) of seats of the Left was alarming.

These were won by the National Unity Front (NUF), a grouping of a number of parties, which received 30 percent of the popular vote. U Nu, disturbed over the results, temporarily resigned as prime minister in June 1956, resolving to reorganize the party within a year. U Ba Swe became prime minister and U Kyaw Nyein deputy prime minister. U Nu returned to office in March 1957, his task incomplete.

Although there were minor doctrinal differences between the leaders (for example, U Ba Swe felt Marxism and Buddhism were compatible; U Nu thought they were not), their general orientation was toward broadly based democratic socialism and the extension of social services to the widest possible population. The tensions that developed were over relatively minor points of policy, but they grew as such grievances accumulated. More importantly, they were concentrated on the division of power and the spoils of leadership and patronage within the AFPFL and the government. This situation was not new. Burmese politics under the modest degree of autonomy the British granted in the last phase of colonial rule was also characterized by factionalism and personal rivalries.

The choice of a secretary for the AFPFL was the climax of these internecine struggles. U Nu, a political pragmatist, consistently reached for the broadest political support regardless of ideology or other factors. Thus, backed by Thakin Tin and the peasants' organization, he picked Thakin Kyaw Dun, a peasant organizer with an unsavory reputation, against the wishes of Ba Swe and Kyaw Nyein. The formal split of the once all-powerful AFPFL occurred in 1958 and this rivalry engendered the first military, caretaker government.

SOCIALISM AND THE PLANNING PROCESS, 1948–1958

The economic policies followed by the British in Burma were essentially laissez-faire, except when explosively deteriorating conditions, such as spreading tenancy and anti-Indian riots, finally forced the government to intervene. They did so halfheartedly. Central planning first came to Burma in the wake of a war-devastated economy. In 1946, in order to rebuild the destroyed cities and towns, a National Planning Department was created, but its responsibilities soon were broadened beyond urban renewal to consideration of wider economic and social goals as these became recognized. Experts estimated the costs of reconstruction in the postwar era at $3 billion.

The structure of postwar and postcolonial Burma was discussed in 1947 at the "Sorrento villa" meeting in Rangoon, which Aung San coordinated. This was followed by the creation of a National Planning Board to prepare an integrated plan for the country, to determine priorities, and to coordinate individual components of the overall plan. This effort aborted after only one meeting, because the assassinations of Aung San and his colleagues in 1947 disrupted government activity.

In late 1947, just prior to independence, an Economic Planning Board was organized. Reporting to the prime minister, its formation was based upon Article 41 of the new constitution, which stipulated that Burma would have a planned economy. The Burmese wanted a planned welfare state with a strong emphasis on the cultural uplift of the people. The first economic plan of the newly independent country, the Two-Year Plan of Economic Development for Burma, was an eclectic mixture of Burmese, British, and Marxist inspiration and was based on the recommendations of the earlier Sorrento meeting. It was more socialist than the constitution. The plan called for a fully socialist economy that would ultimately remove the tension between employers and employed. Capitalistic gain was eschewed. The profit motive would not be allowed to determine economic development in independent Burma.

The economic plan, overly optimistic, was cut short by the insurgencies that spread throughout the country and drove total output down to the 1946–1947 level, a figure that was only 61 percent of that of the prewar period. The plan could not have reached its goals in any case. It was more a statement of economic and social aspirations than a guide for action. It reflected those principles that were at the heart of the nationalist movement, and most of the policies were eventually implemented by later AFPFL governments. None of the targets was reached on schedule, and a decade later most accomplishments still lagged behind planned goals. Rice exports, for example, were supposed to reach 3.18 million tons in 1951/52. They have yet to attain that level in independent Burma.

In the early stages of the planning process several foreigners were involved, among them J. S. Furnivall, who was an adviser to the government on planning. In 1951, a group of Oxford University economists did some preliminary economic analysis. They were followed later in the year by a U.S.-supported team that assisted in the formation of the Eight-Year Plan. A preliminary report was prepared by January 1952, and endorsed by the Pyidawtha Conference that August, although the comprehensive program took two years to write. The Eight-Year Plan was to run from January 1952 to September 1959. Its goal was simply the restoration of the prewar standard of living. Its basic targets, as with the Two-Year Plan before it, were not attained, although in some sectors such as paddy production and rice exports, the targets were more modest. Especially imporant were inflated miscalculations in the rice export price, which in fact fell after the Korean War, thus lowering foreign exchange earnings.

The value of rice exports only reached K856 million in 1959/60, compared to a target of K1,835 million. Total government exports were expected to reach K2,207 million in 1958/59, but in fact were K890 million that year. The resultant shortages of foreign exchange affected the whole economy. Gross capital formation was 20 percent under the target for the public sector, 30 percent short in the private sector.

There was no priority given to agriculture, irrigation, forestry, or mining in the plan (the military later made the same mistake in the 1960s). Instead, the plan stressed transportation, power, industry, and construction. Since the plan was in large part conceived by foreigners, and the Burmese felt that they knew little about agriculture, a separate Five-Year Plan for Agricultural Self-Sufficiency and Development was proposed in 1952.

By 1955, foreign exchange reserves had fallen to K628 million, about half of those in June 1953. The Eight-Year Plan was therefore abandoned. The government attempted to implement those projects within the plan for which funds were available. A new Four-Year Plan was attempted, beginning in 1956. Its purpose was to increase foreign exchange earnings, so it concentrated on agriculture, but rice production fell 300,000 tons short of the target, and foreign exchange increased only K21 million, compared to the goal of K172 million. Various civilian reorganizations of the planning mechanisms had little positive effect. Under the caretaker government they were held in abeyance, for the new military cabinet was appreciably smaller than the civilian one and the military believed it could handle planning without a special bureaucratic mechanism.

Planning under the civilian governments was based on false expectations of the world market, a failure in which the government's foreign advisers must share at least equal responsibility with the Burmese. The neglect of the agricultural sector, first in the Eight-Year Plan and then in subsequent budget allocations, was a major blunder that had the effect of denying to the government the foreign exchange necessary to carry out the remainder of its development program, since rice exports provided over 80 percent of foreign earnings. Although the plans of the AFPFL administration could not be considered as doctrinaire socialism, they were couched in the classical rhetoric of socialist thinking. Based on a perceived need to make Burma an advanced state, they emphasized the industrial sector to the overall detriment of the country. The military, ten years later, was to repeat this mistake.

Planning in the civilian period also failed because of inherent problems of coordination within the bureaucracy, as well as the lack and ineffective use of trained manpower. Skilled workers were in extremely short supply in the early 1950s; but by the close of the civilian period in 1962, Burma could not absorb the highly trained technicians who were emerging from Burmese and foreign institutions. Planning problems were thus exacerbated by the misuse of available manpower and the inattention given to streamlining the administrative aspects of government planning.

Because planning was a product of the socialist intellectual environment that permeated Burmese thought, the private sector was constantly denigrated in the planning process. Planning started in the classic socialist mold; but with the pragmatism that became a hallmark of Burmese efforts, it began to shift in 1955 when it became obvious that the Eight-Year Plan was a failure. On June 8, 1955, the government publicly announced a change in emphasis to the private sector, guaranteeing private investment free of nationalization for a minimum of ten years and allowing remittances of current earnings and dividends together with repatriation of capital. This well-meaning effort failed, for laws to enforce this policy were never enacted. The policies of Ba Swe in the period of U Nu's retirement continued to emphasize the need for growth in the private sector, but rivalries within the AFPFL resulting in its eventual split and U Nu's reliance on the left-wing NUF prevented any real encouragement of the private sector. With the caretaker government, socialism was again endorsed, but with a military flavor. When U Nu returned to power in 1960, he was again under pressure from the Left, so that a swing to a more liberal economic policy continued to be impossible.

THE MILITARY INTERREGNUM, 1958–1960

The factional struggles that had been so apparent in the AFPFL for many years reached their climax on April 28, 1958. The AFPFL, the single, unifying umbrella political organization that had led the country through the last stages of World War II and through the negotiations with the British for independence, finally and formally split into two. The political aura surrounding the AFPFL designation was still very powerful, so both groups wished to retain the title. U Nu and Thakin Tin headed the "Clean AFPFL" and U Ba Swe and U Kyaw Nyein the "Stable AFPFL." There were little, if any, ideological differences between the two groups. Both had evolved out of the same nationalistic and socialist tradition, and they reflected the mobility and aspirations associated with that heritage.

U Nu continued to be prime minister, but to retain that position he had to promise to assist the Mon and Arakanese minorities to achieve their separate states within the Union. He narrowly won a vote of confidence on June 9, but his majority eroded. On August 19, he passed the annual budget by presidential decree, a legal but unusual action, for he recognized that he did not command sufficient votes in Parliament.

With Buddhist compassion, as well as astute political acumen, U Nu on July 31 offered amnesty to all surrendering insurgents. Some 2,000 came in from the jungle and formed a new leftist group, the People's Comrade party. The position of all left-wing organizations was strengthened because they knew U Nu needed their support. They tried to take advantage of their strength and attempted to place military figures sympathetic to the National Unity Front in key command positions, a move Ne Win and the senior military leadership opposed.

Tensions inexorably soared toward the scheduled climax of national elections in November 1958, elections that most likely would have torn the country apart and given the extreme Left opportunities for very substantial gains, both through the legal party structure and through the insurgencies. At that point, a curious event brought the military to power for the first time. The leadership of the military directly under Ne Win met with U Nu. From that meeting came agreement that U Nu would formally request the military, through appropriate constitutional procedures, to form a caretaker government until the time elections could be held. Initially they were scheduled for April 1959. This procedure seemed agreeable to both factions of the AFPFL, for neither expected to receive a majority in an early election. The negotiations, to which U Nu had to accede, were called by some a "coup by consent" or a "constitutional coup d'état."

U Nu and the military adhered to constitutional procedures and the military did not take over the government until a month later, but there was no question that a coup, albeit a nonviolent one in which the incumbent government cooperated, had taken place. In fact, for some years there had been growing discontent among some military officers over civilian mismanagement of the economy. This crisis gave at least some in the military the excuse for action they had long sought.

The military, on the termination of their caretaker government, compared their accomplishments with those of Hercules cleaning the Augean stables. Although the comparison with Hercules may be considered hyperbole, there is no doubt that their accomplishments were impressive and that they had attained their short-term goals: the reestablishment of law and order, the destruction of illegal economic activities, and the preparation for civilian elections. The growth of confidence among the military in their own capacity to administer and to deal with the vital economic issues facing the state was to become the backdrop to the successful military coup of 1962. The Burmese came to economics from an unusual position. Virtually excluded from the military under the British, they were politicians first—"socialists who became soldiers not soldiers who became socialists." This distinction may help explain the vigor of their economic doctrine following the coup.

The method by which the military sought to accomplish their goals was simple and direct: they seconded military officers to each ministry or department to take over the functions of management. Unlike the civilian governments, there was no need to consider the political implications of each act; the left wing had no leverage over army decisions. The military ruled autocratically, if constitutionally. Political activity was halted and the military concentrated on establishing law and order internally and on launching operations against the insurgents.

The army did succeed in lowering the crime rate, arresting more than four times more "economic insurgents" than the previous government, and actually bringing far more of them to trial. Extensive operations were conducted against the 15,000 insurgents of all colors and denominations. The military claimed that the rebels were on the brink of collapse. This claim proved erroneous. The rebels were contained, although increased insurgent activity broke out in the Shan State after the military had negotiated the settlement of the traditional authority of the *sawbwas* of that region. The military also established three satellite towns in the rice fields around Rangoon—North and South Okkalappa and Thaketa—to which they moved over 167,000 squatters who had gradually inundated Rangoon. The army claimed that these squatters had been used by various politicians for their own ends. There was no appeal from this forced exodus.

The government attacked economic problems in a dual manner. First, they set about lowering prices in the bazaars by fiat and increased the supply of commodities enough to force prices down, thereby improving the distribution of many consumer goods. Second, and more important for the long term, they expanded the Defense Services Institute (DSI). This military-run organization, which had started as a sort of post exchange, expanded into thirteen specialized economic organizations and became, in effect, a military conglomerate. It ran an external shipping line, a bank, a department store, trading groups, hotels, and an electronic works. The objective of DSI was thus transformed from that of supplying goods to military personnel to affecting the whole economy both by lowering prices and by expanding the competence of the Burmese (as opposed to Indian and Chinese businessmen) in economic fields. Following the return to civilian rule, the DSI was transformed into the Burma Economic Development Corporation, run by the military in mufti.

The achievements of that period extended beyond domestic matters. Ne Win journeyed to Peking and completed a long-negotiated border agreement with the People's Republic of China. Burma seemed once again on the road to stability. The army was impressed with the Israeli military and adapted several Israeli programs. Universal conscription was passed for both men and women (but never enforced), and the Burmese transformed the concept of a military kibbutz into a resettlement program for the army in which veterans were located on extensive farming areas at strategic locations in the Shan and Kachin states.

The military had set forth their priorities. They wanted to reestablish law and order first, to promote democracy second, and to develop a socialist economy third. In their next bureaucratic incarnation in 1962 they eliminated the second priority.

THE TRIUMPH OF U NU

Originally the election was scheduled to be held by April 1959. This would have given the caretaker government about six months in which to restore order and prepare the nation for voting. The military agenda, however, was larger than perhaps anyone had anticipated and required more time. The politicians also were not ready to compete, for their organizational work was just beginning. By mutual agreement and in accordance with parliamentary procedures the elections were postponed until February 1960.

The military had close ties with U Ba Swe and U Kyaw Nyein, two men who had held high office and had worked with the military in the past. They felt that these men had pragmatic approaches to economics and politics, were tough-minded on national issues, and did not, like U Nu, spend what the army regarded as an inordinate amount of time in meditation. They, rather than U Nu, would be able to stand up against minority demands for more ethnic states or greater autonomy for those groups and would not allow the left wing to infiltrate the government. Thus the military subtly furthered the campaign of the Stable AFPFL.

In the meantime, U Nu and his colleagues had transformed the Clean AFPFL into a new party, the Pyidaungsu (Union) party. As the campaign got under way, U Nu capitalized on his real interest in Buddhism, which was, of course, the religion of about 85 percent of the population. He had many monks and *sangha* organizations working for him (one also campaigned for the Stable AFPFL); he chose the saffron color of the Buddhist monks' robes as his official campaign color; and on the ballot box (each party had a separate box), he had his picture placed, which some said could hypnotize the voters. U Nu was to many a devout, almost what a Westerner might call a saint. He promised states to the Mon and the Arakanese, and he said he would pass a constitutional amendment making Buddhism the state religion.

The results of the election were clear — U Nu and the Union party won an overwhelming victory, much to the army's chagrin. His party received two-thirds of the vote and 159 seats in the 250-seat Chamber of Deputies, compared to 41 for the Stable AFPFL. As they had promised, the military relinquished power, returned to the barracks, and allowed the newly reformed government to begin the difficult task of reformulating national policy. They had tasted power, however, and acquired confidence in managing all the affairs of the nation, at least for a short period. By all accounts and for most observers, both Burmese and foreigners, they had done so with credit, dedication, and forcefulness. They had temporarily halted national decay.

U Nu's new government lasted two years, but from the beginning the seeds of its destruction were present. To fulfill his campaign promise, U Nu started the process by which Buddhism could become the state religion. This created much dissension, especially among the Kachin. Unlike the Shan and Kayah, the Kachin had no titular authority to leave the Union and, unlike the Karen, they were not already in revolt. But a significant percentage of them were Christian. They were far more articulate than the animists, and they held mass meetings throughout the Kachin State to denounce the government and U Nu in particular. To assuage the Kachin and other minorities including the Karen, who were scattered throughout Lower Burma and were not in revolt, U Nu also promised that he would pass another constitutional amendment affirming the freedom of religion. This promise somewhat pacified the minorities but angered many Buddhists, including a number of monks who demonstrated against him. In the end, both amendments passed, but at great costs to the country and to little practical effect.

In the meantime the Shan were meeting to discuss their future within and without the Union. Typifying Burmese politics, U Nu's Union party was splitting into factions that once again threatened that party as a cohesive unit. As pressures built up, the prime minister was forced to consider the protestations of his own left wing, which was becoming more vehement. The year 1961 ended on disquieting notes.

5

Military Rule in Burma, 1962–1980

The Burma army had demonstrated its administrative competence between 1958 and 1960, as well as its dedication to the nation. It is not surprising that the political deterioration after the elections of 1960 prompted a military response.

THE COUP: ORIGINS AND EFFECTS

By 1961 minority tensions had built to a crescendo. On August 26, Parliament passed the constitutional amendment making Buddhism the state religion. It exacerbated friction between the dominant Buddhist Burmans and the Kachin and Karen, a substantial minority of whom were Christian. The military opposed the bill because they recognized the increased danger to the already fragile union, plagued by minority insurrections. Minimally, they wanted the legislation limited to Burma Proper, the Burman Buddhist heartland.

For the Buddhist Shan there were other, more structural, problems. They felt discriminated against, both economically and socially. Of all the minorities except the Mon, they alone had evolved a complex, sophisticated, and hierarchical political system. They wanted a greater share of the union financial pie and a more equitable distribution of foreign assistance, in accordance with their population and natural resource base. Increasingly discontent, thirty-three Shan leaders met in February 1961 in Taunggyi, the capital of their state, to discuss their legal, but unrealistic, option of leaving the Union of Burma, a theoretical possibility under the provisions of the 1947 constitution. Some of them advocated increased autonomy within the Union; others wanted independence. At the close of their meeting, they formed a Constitutional Revision Steering Committee to continue consideration of their future. A year later in late February 1962, the Shan *sawbwas*, together with some Kayah leaders (representing a state with the same legal option) assembled again, this time in Rangoon, to continue their deliberations from the previous year.

Meanwhile, U Nu, under pressure from the political Left, agreed in January 1962 to the nationalization of all import firms. These companies, mainly Burmese, vied to obtain lucrative import licenses, many of which they sold to foreign – usually Indian – establishments. State ownership, planned to begin March 1, would have hastened the process of Burmanization. Politically desirable for any government, it would have undercut the economic position of the highly entrepreneurial minorities. Perhaps more importantly, it would have eliminated the importing functions of the Burma Economic Development Corporation (the old Defense Services Institute), the military-owned conglomerate that had assumed a major economic role since the caretaker government. Nationalization would also have given one faction of U Nu's Union party, the so-called Thakin faction, a financially secure means of perpetuating its political power, thus exacerbating tensions within that structure.

On March 2, to the surprise of most people – even many highly placed – Burma underwent a radical change. Early in the morning the military swiftly and almost bloodlessly (one life was lost) carried out an efficient coup d'état. The army arrested the president, the prime minister, members of the cabinet, and justices of the court, together with all the Shan and Kayah leaders who were assembled in Rangoon for their meeting. Ne Win, as commander of the armed forces and coup leader, declared that the coup was necessary to preserve the Union. A seventeen-man Revolutionary Council, all of whom were key military figures led by Ne Win, was installed and began to rule by decree. On March 9 the Revolutionary Council invested Ne Win with full executive, legislative, and judicial authority. He retained that power until March 2, 1974, twelve years to the day after the coup. Then a new national assembly took office under a new constitution. However, Ne Win continued effectively to wield power, if not by virtue of his role as sole authority in the administrative structure, then because of his personal prestige and paramount position.

The Revolutionary Council in 1962 eliminated all legal barriers to military rule, the essential purpose behind the arrest of the leading central government officials. In subsequent actions the council suspended the constitution and dissolved Parliament on March 3 and dissolved the high and supreme courts on March 20. The military had assumed complete control. There was no threat, military or judicial, to their position.

The precipitating cause of the coup and its timing seem rooted in the growing fear that the Shan State might attempt to leave Burma, although the preservation of the military's role in the economic sphere may have contributed to the sense of urgency. As a result of the army's positive experience during the caretaker government, however, there was confidence within the ranks in the ability of their leaders, enabling them to take unified action. If the military could slow, at least temporarily, the earlier economic, administrative, and political decline felt in 1958, then they surely could run the nation in 1962.

Military rule brought critical changes to Burma: some were almost immediate, whereas others slowly gestated. With these changes, attitudes toward the coup shifted. In some quarters, army authority was first greeted with a sense of relief, for the caretaker period, in spite of the autocratic exercise of power, was a productive eighteen months.

The public was at first lulled. Economically and politically, the Revolutionary Council moved slowly. Secure in their military and executive positions, the members first attempted to co-opt and cajole, rather than dictate. Political parties were not immediately banned. Their cooperation was sought. The press was restrained, but not completely controlled. Early statements in the days following the coup were moderate. Yet underlying this moderation and behind the public facade were the beginnings of a new and more vigorous emphasis on socialism. The National Unity Front, a left-wing party, threw its support behind the military within days, perhaps because it had nowhere else to go, but also perhaps because it recognized the direction the regime would take.

Almost immediately after the coup, the new regime began to formulate the ideological basis for the future direction of the state. Three critical documents were hurriedly completed. The first of these, *The Burmese Way to Socialism*, published on April 30, proclaimed the revitalization of the socialist goal and discarded parliamentary democracy, which it said had failed. It called for state ownership of the means of production. It reflected the mainstream of modern Burmese thought—nationalism and socialism. One eminent Burman, Dr. Ba Maw, summed it up: because it was socialist it was good, but because it was Burmese it was better.

On July 4, the Burma Socialist Programme party (BSPP) was founded and its constitution, the second critical document, was published. The party, formed initially as a cadre organization for an indefinite but transitional period, was modeled on eastern European parties and constituted on the basis of democratic centralism. It took almost a decade to shed its transitional cadre chrysalis and become a mass party. It was twelve years before its legal status as the only recognized political entity was formalized under a new constitution.

On January 17, 1963, the last of the trilogy appeared. *The System of the Correlation of Man and His Environment (The Philosophy of the BSPP)* is the quintessential Burmese paper. Providing the philosophical underpinnings for *The Burmese Way to Socialism* and the rationale for the monopolistic political aspects of the party, it was an eclectic mixture of Marxism and Buddhism, and distinctly Burmese. It rejected historical determinism. It regarded all things as in a state of flux. It was humanistic, concentrating on man, not ideology. It rejected the "vulgar materialism" of the Left and the Right. It proclaimed its own fallibility, noting that party dogma and programs could also change, and it specifically advocated ideological flexibility in enabling the military to meet the problems that the regime would later encounter. It explicitly stated that all party doctrines and programs could be revised. Even the party's revealed truth was relative.

These three documents together formed the basis for the distribution of political and economic power. Curiously, as interpreted by the party leadership over two decades, these documents supported flexibility in economic planning, but rigidity in political structure. Taken as a whole, they articulated the goals of the state, the philosophical bases for such goals, and the administrative means by which the goals were to be achieved. Few regimes have been as thorough or as efficient in their timely expression of such a holistic system. Whatever the papers may have lacked in philosophical precision, they made up in breadth of vision. They clearly were in the Burmese tradition, appealing to and melding the three central concepts in modern Burman life – nationalism, socialism, and Buddhism. Yet the indigenous tradition they reflected was more Burman than Burmese. The document describing the goals of the state could have been more aptly called *The Burman Way to Socialism*.

The early persuasive, rather than coercive, policies of the Revolutionary Council in economics and politics quickly ended. Perhaps the hectic, almost frantic, pace of preparation of *The Burmese Way to Socialism* after the coup and the formulation of the BSPP crystallized military sentiment in the direction of swift progress along a particularly Burmese road to socialism. Another key reason may have been the violent student demonstrations that broke out against the more stringent hostel regulations at the University of Rangoon, culminating on July 7, 1962, in an incident in which the military fired on the students, killing many, some say hundreds. The following day the army-ordered demolition of the Rangoon University Student Union building, a gratuitous and unnecessary act, obliterated an important symbol of Burmese nationalism since the 1930s. It had been as familiar a symbol in the secular sphere as the Shwedagon Pagoda was a symbol of Buddhism and nationalism in the religious. As a result, public opinion shifted, turning against the government. The student demonstrations and their tragic aftermath were harbingers of the continuous trouble the military experienced from the volatile student community.

THE FIRST DECADE: ECONOMICS

The Burmese Way to Socialism defined the ultimate goals for the Burmese state, but it specified neither the timing nor the emphases needed to achieve those goals. Since all Burmese governments after independence had been socialist to some degree, the first few months were reassuring. Brigadier Aung Gyi, the unannounced heir apparent to Ne Win, spoke moderately, emphasizing agriculture – the prime national asset. In February 1963, he was replaced, and the government took a more strident socialist approach with an increased program of nationalization. The shift paralleled the rise to power of Brigadier Tin Pe, a more orthodox Marxist.

Foreign firms, not unexpectedly, were the first to feel the effects of the new policies, for Burmanization of the economy had been a prime requisite of political action since independence. The first to go was Imperial Chemical Industries on August 1, 1962, followed by the Burma Oil Company on January 1, 1963. The tempo accelerated. The following month, with the ouster of Aung Gyi, all foreign and private banks were nationalized. That same month the Revolutionary Council announced that all major industries would also be taken over by June 1, 1963. At that time, Ne Win stipulated that the state would nationalize the production, distribution, import, and export of all major commodities and prohibit the formation of new private industries. The government was determined to limit the private sector to retail trade, and even that field was undercut by the development of people's stores that sold staples (when available) at controlled prices.

Shifts in regulations did occur (more stringent ones were replaced by ones somewhat less pervasive as implementation faltered and economic chaos seemed near). The overall economic direction, however, was clear: state ownership of the basic means of production was extended as far as, and often beyond, the administrative reach of the government. Not only was private investment of any sort discouraged, but private funds were rooted out in the belief that many of them were in foreign hands and that the old elite should be deprived of power. In May 1964, K50 and K100 notes, the largest currency denominations, were demonetized, forcing large amounts of cash (about K1 billion) out of private control. Taxation of saving accounts and safe deposit boxes effectively precluded accumulation of private capital for production and investment. Whatever savings existed thereafter were in the time-honored forms of gold or jewelry. Some 15,000 enterprises, large and small, were nationalized. Currency regulations and trade and production restrictions forced around 200,000 noncitizen Indians and Pakistanis, some of whom had lived in Burma for decades, to leave the country without their assets.

Because they had controlled much of the retail and wholesale trade, they had become objects of national antipathy, which since the 1930s occasionally took a violent form. In April 1964, the government established a Socialist Economic Construction Committee to run major businesses.

The nationalization of the industry and trade was but one plank in the construction of a socialist state. For the Burmese, another was the stress on developing heavy industries. Following a doctrinaire socialist path, the government seemed bent on creating an industrial proletariat. During this decade, perhaps K1 billion ($213 million) was invested in the expansion of Burmese industry. In 1961, only 3.6 percent of capital investment was in industry, but by 1971 it was 37 percent. In spite of what for Burma was a massive infusion of funds, value added in industry increased by only 2.6 percent per year, and the value of industrial production rose by 4.6 percent in constant prices. Industry's share of gross domestic production remained constant at 10 percent, and volume increased at less than 1 percent per year, falling behind rises in population. Factories mushroomed. The nationalized industrial share of the processing and manufacturing sector rose from 31.6 percent in 1962/63 to 46.4 percent in 1977/78. In spite of this emphasis, the private sector, small-scale and fragmented, remained eleven times the size of the public sector and employed ten times the number of people. Yet, in the Rangoon Division, where the bulk of industry was located (in 1979 one-half of the industrial target was situated there), the number of private firms declined precipitously. In 1963 there were 493 firms (excluding handicrafts) employing 17,947 persons; by 1972 there were 276 firms providing work for 6,887 people and the value of production had fallen in half.

Industrial strategy was based on an import-substitution model. The attempted expansion of large numbers of new factories to attain this goal was ill-conceived and poorly executed. More attention was paid to new plants than to improvement of existing facilities. Few industries operated at anything near capacity, with some at as little as one-third of maximum production. Local raw materials were not available for some plants; foreign exchange was not allocated to others. Industry was decapitalized, for funds were not budgeted for spare parts and required commodities; depreciation was not calculated. Management was centralized, prices controlled, and worker productivity fell. Even more importantly, the government erred in its priorities. Instead of capitalizing on Burma's position in agriculture – the basis of Burma's greatest past and potential wealth – and on forestry and mining, including oil production, the government stressed the country's weakest point – industry. It was a mistake that the government later rectified, at least in part, but for the first decade government policy had disastrous effects.

For the period from 1961 to 1973, paddy production grew from

6.726 million tons to 7.261 million tons, but the population grew by about 25 percent. Rice exports were 1.676 million tons in 1961, but they dropped to 0.715 million tons by 1971 and were only worth $23.3 million that latter year. Burma was in serious trouble.

Ironically, as the military hastened to control the whole economy and expand the role of the state sector, it began to purge from its meager corps of seasoned administrators those who, more than all others, might have managed the increasingly complex public sector. Many senior military officers who had been successful during the caretaker period lost political favor and thus their jobs. The Revolutionary Council also retired about 2,000 career civil servants. These officers, some of whom had been in the upper ranks of the British-sponsored elite Burma Civil Service, were suspect as remnants of the colonial status quo. They were called effete by the military; yet their bureaucratic skills might have helped the system work.

With state control, corruption expanded. Consumer goods production fell, and imports of these commodities dropped. But the population kept rising and with it demand. The unavailability of even the most common necessities, such as clothing, soap, medicines, cooking oil, or kerosene and the high food prices worked together to cause the expansion of an already pervasive black market. There were twenty-three government corporations—the black market became known as Corporation 24. Private capital, what little existed, had few legal avenues of economic investment. If money had to be made, the easiest ways to do so were through smuggling of consumer goods, the internal and illegal exchange of such commodities as well as those produced in Burma and in short supply, and the illegal export of both raw materials—such as jade, precious stones, teak—and other goods such as antiques. So efficient was the process that antiques could be ordered from Burma in Bangkok and delivered in record time. The government's early attempts to control the trade failed. Thereafter, there was essentially studied ignorance of its existence, with a few minor efforts basically for show. The trade also provided needed income to civil servants, whose salaries were still at 1948 levels. Corruption became the counterpoise of ideological rigidity and a failing bureaucracy.

THE FIRST DECADE: POLITICAL CONTROL

The Burma Socialist Programme party (BSPP) was the Revolutionary Council in mufti. For over nine years, until it finally passed in 1971 from a cadre to a mass organization, it contained at its largest only twenty-four full members, thirteen of whom were also members of the Revolutionary Council.

The BSPP, under its transitional constitution of 1962, was meant to be transformed. The problem Ne Win faced was how to keep control over this incipient political tool that was to perpetuate his military revolution until the party could be institutionalized as the national political force, ensuring his continued domination of the nation. The means were cleverly contrived. By first keeping membership small and confining it to his military subordinates – his personal entourage – and to a few trustworthy civilians, he was able to control the cadre party. By opening potential membership to others selectively, primarily as "candidates" for membership and as party "sympathizers," he could expand the party at will into a mass movement yet continue to assure control.

To retain command, Ne Win recruited potential party members in great numbers from the *tatmadaw,* the military, thus perpetuating his control both through the party hierarchy and the military command structure. At the time of the conversion of the BSPP to a mass organization, there were 73,369 members, 58 percent of whom were in the military or were formerly in that group. Of 260,857 candidate members, 24.4 percent were also from the armed forces. Conversely, two-thirds of the armed forces of Burma were either full party members or candidates; yet the military constituted about 0.5 percent of the total population.

The party mechanism spread throughout the country. In each of the 314 townships in the nation there was either a party unit or a party organizing committee, but there were 338 such committees at the battalion or lower military level and 13 at the military command level. In 1971, a party central committee was organized with 150 members, of whom 127 were from the armed services.

Political control could be maintained by military force, but political indoctrination and the capacity to mobilize large numbers of people to support state objectives were required. During the first decade the party planned and slowly expanded a series of integrated mass organizations designed to service party needs and to reach all points in the nation over which the government maintained control.

No group was ignored. All those over five years old were potential members of one or another group, if they could meet the entrance qualifications. Three party youth organizations were formed. Each had its special age cohort, together spanning the five- to twenty-five-year old age groups. By January 1981, they totaled over 5.1 million members, or about 15 percent of the total population.

The military divided the general population into workers or peasants, the latter being far more numerous in this agrarian society. Under the party, each category was a potential member of a workers' or peasants' council (later named an *asiayone,* or "association"). By 1980, after careful organizational work, the peasants' *asiayone* had 7.6 million members. In contrast, the workers' *asiayone* numbered 1.5 million. The government also tried to bring specialized interests under direct supervision. The military tried to register the approximately 100,000 to 150,000 monks in the Buddhist *sangha* in 1965. It failed then, because of demonstrations, but it may have succeeded in 1980. (In March 1982, the state announced that 160,845 monks were registered.) Literary and intellectual organizations were proposed, but they took longer to become active. It was not until 1980 that the Federation of Literary Workers was established, although planning had begun in 1965.

The masses were organized into one or another of the party-sponsored organizations, until perhaps one out of every three noninfants in government controlled areas was at least formally a member of one or another group. The elite was not ignored. Several important training centers were also founded to inculcate party ideals in the bureaucracy and in the army. These included the Central School of Political Science (later the Institute of Political Science), the Academy for the Development of National Groups, and a series of military-run centers. Tens of thousands of civilians and military personnel passed through these institutions. The official trilogy was often a required part of the various curricula.

All of these mechanisms were used to persuade, cajole, or enforce mass participation in nationally mandated programs, including meeting paddy procurement quotas, cleaning the streets, raising productivity, building roads or health centers, and involvement in the antinarcotics and other campaigns. How effective any of these groups would be without the prospect of coercion is, of course, not known. If these were the positive means to enforce or persuade, there were negative factors at work as well.

Soon after assuming power, the military sought to shut Burma off from the outside world. Foreign information organizations were banned and foreign educational and cultural activities closed. Visas became more restrictive, and reporters were discouraged. The press was censored and then in 1965 taken over. Privately owned newspapers and magazines were either closed or nationalized. Foreign schools, often supported by missionaries, became government institutions; missionaries, once they had left Burma, were not permitted to return. Tourism dwindled for visas were good for only twenty-four hours.

Shut off externally and under the military's rigid internal control, Burma turned inward to try to find the route to Burmese socialism. In pursuing this course, the military had transformed the nation. Since independence Burma had been a relatively classless society with social mobility much in evidence. The educational institutions, the military, politics, and the monkhood all offered opportunities. By co-opting politics and placing power in military hands alone, the military dammed the fluidity of Burmese society. Burma was under a rigid ideological cloak in olive drab.

THE FIRST DECADE:
FOREIGN RELATIONS AND DOMESTIC UNREST

The career of U Thant, Burma's most famous citizen, in a sense characterizes Burma's foreign policy. U Nu's personal secretary and later, prior to the military takeover, ambassador to the United Nations, U Thant was in New York at the time of the coup and thus escaped what almost certainly would have been arrest during the early years of the military regime. As an astute, although not intellectual, representative of a country with impeccable neutralist credentials, he became in 1961 acting secretary-general of the United Nations and secretary-general a year later. It was more a testament to Burma's nonaligned foreign policy than to U Thant's personal qualifications. His death and burial in Rangoon in 1974 ignited the most intense display of antimilitary rioting that had yet appeared.

The military continued the foreign policy of predecessor governments. Ne Win was no stranger to international negotiations and had concluded Burma's most important border agreement with China in 1960, during the caretaker period. The Communist states, especially China and Russia, greeted the socialist program of the BSPP with considerable enthusiasm. During the first few years of military rule, numerous high-level Chinese and Russian delegations visited Rangoon. Russian and Chinese economic aid to the new government continued, the latter under a 1961 agreement negotiated after the border settlement. Eastern European nations also provided considerable support.

Burma's relations with its other neighbors were proper, but restrained. Indian and Pakistani ministerial visits took place, and border agreements with both nations secured the western frontier of Burma. The exodus of tens of thousands of Indians and Pakistanis as the Burmanization program intensified and high denomination currency notes were withdrawn strained cordiality, but there was no break in relations. Thailand viewed the development of a strongly socialist state in Burma with considerable alarm. Always fearful of a left-wing regime to its west, and with a war in Indochina to its east, the Thai were concerned that a militant leftist government in Rangoon could destabilize some of the frontier areas. The Thai military leadership quietly acquiesced to ignoring Karen rebel activities and illegal trade along the frontier. It still harbors remnant KMT forces in northern Thailand and other insurgent and warlord groups from the Shan and Kachin states. Thailand gave U Nu political asylum in 1969, from which U Nu unsuccessfully attempted to launch a military offensive to overthrow Ne Win. Thai officials studiously ignored the massive trade in Burmese opium that was exported from Bangkok.

. Relations with the United States and Great Britain cooled. The closure of the U.S. Information Agency Library and the binational center, the termination of the British Council program, and the expulsion of the Ford and Asia foundations all enhanced the impression, to which the new political structure and economic program contributed, of a leftward swing under a neutralist guise. In spite of this, U.S. official economic aid continued with new projects. It was gradually phased out after 1966. Japan became the mainstay of foreign assistance to the military, continuing a low-key but critically important foreign assistance program begun under the civilian governments as war reparations. Burma also relied on UN and Colombo Plan aid, but terminated the assistance of the World Bank and refused to join the Asian Development Bank when it was formed.

The military coup heightened minority frustration. Increased violence and insurrections broke out in the Shan and Kachin states, and the Karen revolt, active since 1949, intensified. Both the Red Flag and White Flag rebellions continued. Rebel groups in the Shan and Kachin areas financed their military campaigns by smuggling opium out of Burma through Thailand to the West, especially to the United States where there was a growing demand for it in the form of heroin.

To head off problems with the multitude of insurrections, Ne Win offered in April 1963 a general amnesty to all insurgents who surrendered. Negotiations with some leaders took place in Rangoon, but overall the amnesty was not a success and only one Karen group came in from the jungle. A cease-fire was the only temporary result. Other amnesties were attempted again in 1974, on the occasion of the new constitution, and in 1980, but with limited effect.

In June 1967, the Chinese Cultural Revolution spilled over into Burma with dire effects on Sino-Burmese relations. Chinese students in Rangoon, inspired by their brethren in China, attempted to wear Maoist badges, an act prohibited by the Burmese authorities. Riots took place, and martial law was declared. The Burmese vented their anger and frustration over internal economic conditions on the Chinese merchants, who generally congregated in one section of downtown Rangoon, and accused them of hoarding goods and raising prices in a time of scarcity. The military may not have been unhappy to see a foreign focus for internal economic anger that had grown as a result of the economic nationalization program.

Peking responded to the dozens of deaths from the riots by attacking the Burmese government as "counterrevolutionary, fascist, and reactionary." Before this period, there is little evidence that the Chinese had assisted the Burma Communist party (White Flag) in its insurrection except to provide training for some of its key leaders. However, the change in Peking's attitudes toward the military, the assassination in September 1968 of BCP leader Thakin Than Tun, and the military defeat of the party in Burma Proper gave the Chinese reason to expand their assistance as the BCP retreated to the remote Wa State area on the China border. Chinese support for some Kachin insurgents also increased at this time. As the riots gave way to verbal exchanges, the foreign focus for the unrest did not last long. Something had to be done about the worsening economy.

At the first BSPP Party Seminar in 1965 Ne Win had noted that economic "conditions worsened to such an extent that the people would have starved if Burma were not a food-surplus country." By August 1967 workers were demonstrating over rice shortages, and the military fired into rioting crowds. Deteriorating economic conditions prompted the army to reassess its economic program. It used the forum of the first BSPP congress, a critical political event. The congress ratified a new economic policy and began activities that revised the administrative and legal structures of the state.

THE FIRST PARTY CONGRESS: POLITICAL AND ECONOMIC CHANGE

Ne Win was not successful in solving the problems associated with the insurgencies. They were a drain on government resources; however they posed no immediate threat to the integrity of the regime or to Ne Win's political power. He had cleverly maintained his authority over the Burma Socialist Programme party in its cadre stage; and by gradually packing its ranks with military personnel, he retained his authority throughout the party's expansion process. Four other problems required solution, however. The first was to overcome economic stagnation and its corrosive effects on his political objectives, the second to establish an orderly system for political succession, the third to institutionalize the BSPP as the sole legal heir to political authority, and the fourth to resolve in some manner the minority problems by redefining the administrative relationships between the minorities and the Burman majority. The first steps toward solution were taken at the First Party Congress of the BSPP, which met in Rangoon between June 28 and July 11, 1971, with over 1,200 delegates in attendance. It marked the formal recognition of the BSPP as a mass organization.

A major item on the agenda of this congress was a remarkable document that was to change Burmese economic policy within the context of the socialist tradition and policy. Economic discontent had already prompted reconsideration of economic issues. The document presented at the congress, *The Long-Term and Short-Term Economic Policies of the Burma Socialist Programme Party,* was a candid expression of economic disillusionment with poor management, if not with socialist goals. It marked the formal beginning of long-term Burmese economic planning. The paper called for the formulation of a Twenty-Year Plan, by the end of which Burma would have become a socialist state. The plan was to be composed of five four-year plans, each building upon the last, so that by 1994, with a two-year delay, Burma would be an industrialized socialist state. Over these two decades, public sector contributions to the national economy were to rise from 36 percent to 48 percent and the cooperative sector from 3 percent to 26 percent, while the private sector contribution was supposed to drop from 61 percent to 26 percent. The GDP growth rate was set at 5.9 percent per year, with annual increases of 4.8 percent in agriculture and 9.4 percent in industry. During the plan period, living standards were to double, and at the end of the plan the private sector, which had control over virtually all agriculture, was to constitute only 40 percent of it, the state sector was to grow to 10 percent, and half of the agricultural economy was to be in the hands of cooperatives.

Skeptics may view the plan as a collection of pious socialist platitudes, but the paper reassessed national priorities and also began the process of reallocating resources. Heavy industry was no longer to be the means by which socialism would be achieved. First priority shifted to those elements of the economy in which Burma had a natural advantage: agriculture, fisheries, livestock, and forestry. Mineral production, virtually ignored in the past, was once again important. Finally, the long suffering consumer was to benefit from production increases.

In addition to shifts in priorities, the paper called for the commercialization of the state enterprises and the payment of incentives to those organizations and individuals who performed well. Altruism was no longer considered sufficient to ensure growth. There was also recognition that the private sector had been slighted. The paper noted that because of the neglect of guidelines for the private sector, employment was stagnating there, while the government lacked the resources to increase public employment or production. As a result, both unemployment and black market trade increased.

Finally, the paper reversed Burmese isolation. Burma had remained neutralist in foreign political relations, but essentially isolationist in economic relations, causing foreign economic support to deteriorate. A new emphasis had to be placed on improving Burma's foreign aid picture.

The Central Committee of the BSPP approved the paper in November 1972, and thereafter, slowly and haltingly, economic changes
were made. Burma invited the World Bank back into the country and
joined the Asian Development Bank. Its efforts to secure foreign
assistance began to bear fruit. There were also critical tax and paddy procurement reforms, economic authority was delegated more easily, and
managers of state industries gained more control over their operations.

Progress was slow. It was one thing to revise priorities and man-
date change; it was quite another to expect a subservient bureaucracy,
the existence of which had depended upon ideological conformity to doctrinaire policies, to respond effectively to such sweeping liberalization.
The economic record, however, had been poor, so positive changes were
relatively easy to introduce. For example, annual growth in the gross
domestic product between 1960 and 1975 was only 1 percent, but the
population had been expanding offficially at a minimum of 2.2 percent
per year.

The First Four-Year Plan (1971/72–1973/74) was a failure and was
truncated. The Second Four-Year Plan (1974/75–1977/78) was far more
successful. It started slowly, with a growth rate of 2.7 percent the first
year and 4.1 percent the second; but by the last year of the plan, growth
was up to a respectable 6.4 percent. Under the Third Four-Year Plan
(1978/79–1981/82), there was marked progress. Growth was 6.5 percent
in 1978/79, 5.4 percent in 1979/80, and 8.3 percent in 1980/81. This progress was due to good rice harvests, vastly expanded planting of the high-
yielding varieties of rice, and much more stringent procurement regulations. There were still structural problems in the economy; however,
performance had improved so much that many of these issues were temporarily masked. The three other problems that Ne Win faced were institutionalizing the process of picking a successor, securing the continued
preeminent position of the BSPP, and trying to solve the minority issues.
All of these problems were addressed in the new constitution.

Immediately following the First Party Congress of the BSPP, the
government announced plans for drafting a new constitution to replace
the 1947 version abrogated by the coup. Thinking about such change
started at least as early as 1969. A ninety-seven-member drafting com-
mission was established. General San Yu, secretary to the BSPP and
shortly thereafter appointed as deputy prime minister, was chairman.
The long process of public consultation began. Three drafts were circulated and teams roamed the nation to discuss the provisions of the new
law. Some 18 million people were involved before it was approved by a
plebiscite in December 1973. It was evident from the beginning that the
purpose of the constitution was to enfeoff the BSPP, and thus the army,
with monopolistic political power.

The constitution provides for a political structure that begins at the 13,751 village tracts (or wards in urban areas). Each village tract (composed of more than one natural village) elects a village people's council. In turn the 314 townships also elect a township people's council, and the process is repeated in the seven divisions and seven states. For example, in October 1981 in the third national election under the 1974 constitution, the citizenry elected 475 members of the Pyithu Hluttaw (People's Assembly), 976 representatives at the state and division level, 22,850 members of the township people's councils, and 163,742 members of the urban ward or village tract people's councils.

At the national level, the Pyithu Hluttaw is constitutionally the highest organ of the state. The party selects a single slate of candidates for the Pyithu Hluttaw. Most, if not all, candidates are affiliated with the party or approved by it. From its membership, the Pyithu Hluttaw elects a twenty-nine member Council of State, the chairman of which becomes the president of the Union. A Council of Ministers is also elected, with the chairman serving as prime minister. In the same manner councils of people's judges, people's attorneys, and people's inspectors are chosen. Thus, for the first time since the military coup of 1962, there is a prescribed administrative means by which a successor to Ne Win can be selected.

All power—executive, legislative, and judicial—resides in the party. There is no separation of powers within the state. In effect, the elaborate constitutional structure is a means by which the military retains control over all aspects of power within the state. Insofar as President Ne Win continues to control the military and, through the military, the BSPP, he maintains authority over all organs of the state.

The constitution explicitly records the rights and duties of the citizenry. Its detail is exemplary with great care taken to assuage minority sensitivities. These rights are all subject to limitations, however, including prohibition of any action that would undermine the socialist system, lead to disunity, or affront public order or morality. The constitution reinforces, and does not limit, the coercive powers of the central government.

The approved constitution, under which the nation's name became the Socialist Republic of the Union of Burma, is a union in name only. It has become a unitary state with effective power in the hands of the Burman majority at the center. Lip service was paid to minority rights, and three new states were created for the Mon, Chin, and Arakanese, making a total of seven states for the minorities and seven divisions in Burma Proper for the Burmans. The balance is perfect, but the symmetry is illusory. Power effectively resides at the center. Although the constitution was officially approved by 90.19 percent of the 14.7 million voters, only

66 percent of the Shan State voters, 69 percent of the Kachin State electorate, 71 percent of the Kayah State, and 86 percent of the Arakanese voters approved of it. In no part of Burma Proper did approval register less than 92 percent. Thus, the unitary state created under the constitution and designed to solve the minority issue is likely to intensify these difficulties. The Burmans have retained, indeed strengthened, their control over the state and do not seem to have extended any conciliatory gestures to the minorities.

POLITICAL CONDITIONS SINCE 1974

If the constitution was supposed to pacify the nation or solve all national ills, it did not succeed. The newly elected Pyithu Hluttaw was installed on March 2, 1974. By May demonstrations and strikes had broken out over high prices, and in June police fired on workers protesting food shortages, killing many of them. Universities were closed to prevent the spread of disturbances.

Trouble soon exploded again in December 1974, this time with greater intensity. The pretext for the demonstrations, which involved substantial numbers of students and monks, was the obvious government slight concerning burial arrangements for U Thant because of his close association with U Nu. The focus of discontent was in actuality Ne Win and his administration in general. Students tried to bury U Thant's body on the site of the demolished Rangoon University Student Union building and held demonstrations at the Shwedagon Pagoda, both locations highly symbolic in Burmese history. Many of the demonstrators were killed and more were arrested, including a large number of monks. Students rioted again in 1975 and 1976. The military, by this time seriously concerned, summarily executed one of the student leaders, which quieted events on the campuses for a period. Such an act was unprecedented in Burmese history.

There were other more elite threats to the regime as well. In 1976 young army officers unsuccessfully attempted a coup in protest of the socialist system. It later proved necessary to purge the cabinet on both the Right and the Left. Indeed, in November 1977 at an extraordinary meeting, Ne Win unexpectedly lost an election for party chairman. New elections were immediately called, which he won. The threats to Ne Win's position have, before and since, been marginal, however. In contrast to many other heads of state, he has left the country on many occasions for extended periods, seemingly secure in his position.

In 1980, Ne Win, in the manner of Burman monarchs and probably with political objectives in mind, convened the Congregation of the Sangha of All Orders for Purification, Perpetuation, and Propagation of the Sasana. This gathering brought together all sects of Buddhist monks to clarify scriptural problems, to weed out bogus monks, and to solve doctrinal disputes. At the same time, the convener earned great Buddhist merit and was also able to gain approval to register the monks, a long-term goal since his unsuccessful attempt to do so in 1965. In the Buddhist tradition, this congregation was followed by an amnesty. Political prisoners were released, and insurgents had ninety days in which to surrender. Over 2,000 took advantage of this opportunity, but the rebellions continued unabated. U Nu, at Ne Win's personal invitation, returned from exile in India and rededicated himself to his enduring concern – Buddhist activities.

The insurgencies continued, denying to the government perhaps 40 percent of the land mass of the country but a small percentage of the population. Today, as under civilian governments, one-third of the national budget is absorbed by defense. Although the insurgents have been major irritants to the Ne Win government, they could become a cancer to his successor. The regime has never been threatened by either the rebellion of the Burma Communist party on the China border, which aims to overthrow the government, or the ethnic insurgencies seeking greater autonomy or independence. Nevertheless the new political structure has not solved these problems and may in fact exacerbate them. In May 1981, Ne Win announced that following the end of the amnesty, discussions took place between the government and the BCP. They broke down when the BCP insisted on continuing its party organization and maintaining its armed forces as well as its separate administration of its border area.

The BSPP has continued to expand. By January 1981, there were over 1.5 million members and an additional 981,000 friends of the party. They were organized in 17,940 party sections and 113,409 party cells. Women members numbered 225,000. Of the armed forces (some 160,000), over 143,000 were party members, ensuring the continuity of military control.

THE ECONOMY TODAY

The extension of government development programs, the source of funds with which to fight the insurgencies, and the provision of imported consumer goods rest on the vitality of the agricultural sector. Agriculture is at the heart of Burma's potential wealth and productive activity. Only 22 percent of the nation is considered urban, and over two-thirds of the total population is engaged in agriculture. Within the agricultural sector, paddy dominates. The conditions of its production, its availability and price, its export, together with its consumption in its

edible form—rice—control national economic growth, the availability of
foreign exchange, individual prosperity, and political stability. Rice
alone accounts for 72 percent of individual caloric intake and 56 percent
of the protein diet.

Before World War II, Burma was the premier rice-exporting nation in the world, with over 12 million acres under cultivation and a production of 7.8 million tons, of which 3.123 million were exported. Rice
alone represented 46.5 percent of Burma's total export earnings. Even in
the early 1950s, with recovery from war damage and the insurrections
incomplete, Burma controlled 28 percent of the world's rice trade. By
1970, Burma's share was only 2 percent. What caused this change?

In world terms the growth of U.S. rice exports has been an important factor. Although this growth does explain somewhat the drop in
Burma's percentage of the world rice trade, it does not explain the drop
in Burmese exports. In 1961, before the coup, exports from Burma were
1.676 million tons; by 1965 they had dropped to 1.3 million tons, in 1972
to 0.715 million tons, in 1973 to 0.262 million, and in 1975 to a low of
0.166 million tons. By 1980 they had once again climbed to an estimated
0.7 million tons, still far below premilitary and prewar levels.

Rice is subject to the vagaries of weather. Drought and flood limit
production, and both are common in parts of the country. Drought is a
special problem, for only about 15 percent of the land is irrigated, most
of it in central Burma. Irrigation in Burma is a form of crop insurance,
guaranteeing sufficient water for the main crop but rarely enough for
double-cropping. There has been in recent years a definite spurt in yields
per acre and in total production—from 30.5 baskets per acre after independence to 42.8 baskets, with total production in 1980 estimated at
10.5 million tons. This is attributed to the introduction of high-yielding
varieties of rice since 1973, their encouraged and sometimes mandatory
use, and an increase in the local production and general availability of
commercial fertilizers. Burma now produces about 130,000 tons using its
natural gas resources.

Increases in population of about 75 percent between 1940 and
1974 are a partial explanation for the drop in Burmese exports, but an insufficient one, for there is as much arable land lying fallow as there is
under cultivation. More important is the reduction in agricultural labor
in spite of increases in the rural population. There is physical insecurity
in the fields, and labor costs are high in comparison to the fixed price of
paddy. There is therefore more broadcasting of seed. This method ob-
viates the need for transplanting and thus more labor but it also reduces
yields. The major reason for decreasing exports, however, is related to
the paddy procurement price paid to farmers and problems of incentives, the security of tenure, and the availability of agricultural credit.

To some degree the Burmese government has controlled the procurement of paddy since independence. Under civilian governments, the export crop was under centralized control, but under the military more stringent quotas are set. The state procures one-third of the crop both for export and for distribution to the rice deficit areas of Burma – cities, parts of central Burma, and some of the states. The farmer is allowed to retain enough for home consumption, seed, and religious offerings. In 1980 the farmers in 171 of the 314 townships had to sell the remainder to the government at a fixed price. In other townships, he is allowed to sell his small surplus only to consumers and only within his township. The remainder is sold to the government at a fixed national price that varies slightly according to the quality of the product. It is, in effect, a form of taxation that rests heavily on the farmer. The difference between the procurement price paid to the farmer and the export price, minus handling, storage, processing, and transportation, represents one-third of internally generated revenue. Thus, the farmer and foreign assistance finance the industrialization and development schemes of the state. In no non-Communist country in Asia is the farmer's return on rice production so low. The state has placed an unequal burden on the farmer, in return for which it has subsidized his fertilizer and eliminated the foreign landlord. In a country with a weak local administrative capacity, it would be difficult to collect any other tax of any size in rural areas, so this strategy has a certain logic.

After the economic reforms of 1972, the military significantly raised the paddy purchase price, from K425 per 100 baskets in that year to K900 in 1975, with no changes of any magnitude since then. The purchase price of paddy has not kept pace with inflation, which is low by international standards. From 1974 to 1981 it was officially 12 percent but perhaps 30 percent at unofficial prices. Procurement is not voluntary; it is forced. Quotas are set by state or division, township, village, and then individual farm. For example, in 1981 the state planned to procure 180 million baskets (8.28 billion pounds), of which the Irrawaddy Division was expected to provide 37.3 percent, Rangoon Division 13.2 percent, Pegu Division 28.2 percent, and the Sagaing Division 5.9 percent. Procurement is enforced through all of the propaganda and coercive organs of the state. The ultimate power of the state in agriculture rests on its ownership of the land, reiterated under the constitutions of 1947 and 1974. More importantly, under the 1974 constitution, the farmer lacks the right to deed his land to his heirs. The village council – that is, the BSPP – now determines who will farm the land following the death or migration of a farmer, although tradition probably plays a vital role in the decision. In 1978 the government warned farmers that, if they did not adhere to their quotas, the state could take away their right to farm the

land. In effect, the state has replaced the Chettyar as landlord. There is
no indication that it may be any the less rapacious, and although there is
no evidence that the state has done so, the threat is well publicized.

With the destruction of the Chettyar credit mechanisms, Burma
gained more equitable income distribution, but it lost an efficient credit
capacity. The state replaced it, but political pressures corrupted the
system during civilian governments. Politicians promised farmers that
agricultural loans would be written off in return for votes. The military
has expanded credit through a variety of mechanisms, but it has provided seasonal credit only, not long-term credit for major productive improvements in the land. A farmer may receive K70 per acre cash on commodities as an advance on his procurement quota, but these funds are
insufficient to improve his productivity. Even if there were more and
longer-term credit, however, the farmer has no incentive either to increase production or to increase the value of his infrastructure permanently for the threat of state confiscation is ever present. Private productive investment in Burma's greatest asset is effectively discouraged.

Government concern over tenancy, expressed as early as 1884 in
Lower Burma, has been a constant and repetitive theme. Tenancy became especially acute during and following the great depression. The
military supposedly and finally eliminated tenancy through legislation in
1963 and 1965. Yet official figures show that it continued until 1971,
when reporting on it stopped. Although tenancy and private credit are no
longer officially recognized, questions remain as to the degree of rural
debt to private moneylenders and indeed to the perpetuation of informal
types of tenancy.

Mineral production has traditionally been important in Burma.
Under the monarchy, oil was produced from shallow wells under royal
monopolies, and before World War II, Burma was an oil exporter. Since
the economic reforms, the state has stressed oil production and increased
tin and tungsten exports. In 1980, Burma expected to produce 12 million
barrels as well as 10,501 million cubic feet of natural gas. The nation is
considered self-sufficient in oil, but internal consumption is kept ar-
tificially low. Shortages often occur and are likely to increase as consumption rises. Mineral production has never returned to prewar levels.
Causes include the location of mines in insecure areas, antiquated equip-
ment, poor quality ores, and inadequate state management.

Overall, has the life of the average Burmese improved? The
answer is complex, and statistics are scant. Yet it is possible to note that
the per capita income in Burma in constant kyat was K395.3 in 1938/39,
but dropped to a low of K218.1 in 1949 because of the war and rebellions. At the time of the military coup it was K335.4, still below prewar
levels. It did not reach prewar standards until 1976 (K399.6). Officially

available consumer goods are less prevalent than before the coup, but the increased availability of black market products has compensated for the scarcity of products distributed through official channels although at higher prices. The Rangoon consumer price index officially rose from 65.3 in 1963 to 100 in 1972 and to 252.6 in 1979.

Social services have improved, if not as rapidly as official figures indicate. Infant mortality dropped from 252 (per 1,000 live births) in 1951 to 50 in 1978, but in reality there were probably more than 100 deaths per 1,000 live births in 1980. The state has made a credible effort to expand health services to rural areas, to increase literacy (as both a social good and political tool), and to improve access to education. These efforts are given high priority in the rhetoric of development planning, but the allocation of resources has been limited. Population increases, officially calculated at 2.2 percent, are probably significantly higher. Family planning is proscribed.

Burma has now probably the most favorable income distribution of any non-Communist country in Asia. Poverty is widespread, and indeed the vast majority of the population can be considered poor. Great affluence, however, is rare. The elite live at modest levels compared to many other developing societies. Inequities still exist, however, and the farmer is hard pressed, while workers are underpaid. The Burmese are not as well off as their resources might allow, but they have eliminated the great income disparities of some other countries.

6

The Culture of Contemporary Burma

Many distinguished Burmese of the contemporary or classical period have been members of minority groups. Some, such as Shu Maung (who changed his name to Ne Win) and Brigadier Aung Gyi were Sino-Burman. U Raschid, a Burmese of Indian origin, was perhaps the most intellectual member of U Nu's cabinets; another, Goshal, was a leader of the Communist insurgents. The Mon provided a continuous stream of literary talent, writing in Burmese, and have remained in the forefront of the Burmese belles lettres tradition. The first commander of the postindependence Burma army was a Karen. Even in the Burman-Mon wars, a Mon led the Burman forces. The first president of the Union of Burma was a Shan, the third a Karen. The fourth was to have been a Kachin, but the military coup intervened.

In spite of the eminence of many from the minorities, they gained prominence outside their own locale insofar as they identified with the mainstream of Burmese social and political life—the culture of the Burman majority. This was the life of two-thirds of the national population, but it was also the only unifying culture with broad political legitimacy over the area of what is now Burma. Conversely, to be prominent and yet remain outside this Burman-dominated multipartite society meant emigration, either literal or figurative. Indians and Pakistanis emigrated, others went underground in the various rebellions, still more walked out illegally over the Thai or Bangladesh borders, and a small but influential and happy few found niches in international organizations. What, then, is the culture of this group at the center of national life? Does it affect Burma's potential for social and economic growth and its place in the regional and world communities?

These questions are perhaps best answered by focusing on several points that are critical to Burma's future, namely, the elite structure and its formation, the status of women, the role of Buddhism, the intellectual in Burman society, and the continuity of this cultural tradition. Nationalism, a vital force in this configuration, and political ideology have already been explored (see Chapter 3).

Ironically, the essence of contemporary Burman life was probably best described about 100 years ago in a remarkably prescient work, *The Burman: His Life and Notions,* by Shway Yoe, the pseudonym of Sir James George Scott. Many aspects of Burman social life and customs Scott describes remain only marginally altered and may strike the observer as unchanged. Other patterns from the precolonial period, downgraded under British rule, seem to have been strengthened. The Burmese language is more widely used today than at independence. The national dress, the ubiquitous *longyi,* worn by both men and women in different forms and patterns, is still standard among the highest and the lowest at the most formal and informal occasions. Buddhism reaches virtually all Burmans and is practiced with unswerving devotion. The status of women is still relatively high, class structure generally fluid, and the Burmans are even more literate than before colonization. Their literacy level is also higher than that of citizens in many developing societies.

Although Scott describes a social system and behavorial patterns that have generally persisted, the dynamic behind these patterns has sometimes altered. Culture is not encased in aspic. It changes in response to stimuli and produces new manifestations. Burma, as a matter of policy since independence, has consciously attempted to retain the uniqueness of its cultural tradition. It has vigorously opposed the modernization or Westernization of its culture while attempting to introduce economic and political change. Maintaining this delicate balance is a continuing dilemma for many societies and few, if any, have resolved it to their satisfaction. It is one that China and Japan faced in the nineteenth century. The Burmese have pointedly looked to Thailand, especially Bangkok, and have sadly noted the destruction or decay of traditional Thai values. The planned retention of what are considered traditional moral virtues unaffected by the pollution of economic change, development, and international trends may be romantic or unrealistic. Nationalistic governments, however, frequently evoke an idealized or imaginary past to elicit a millennial future. The attempt does, however, verify the high esteem in which the Burmans hold their own tradition. It is a tradition in which the Burman feels comfortable, to which he or she returns if at all possible. Political events of the past two decades have created an exiled Burman community, but there had been no earlier brain drain from Burma, in contrast to so many societies. In spite of government policy, the Burman culture is undergoing evolution, but there is a continuity of the tradition vital to understanding contemporary Burma.

THE ELITE STRUCTURE

When the British replaced the monarchy with colonial rule in 1886 and exiled the king to India, the court hierarchy seemed to collapse and all but disappear. The court and the bureaucracy created to run the country were so dependent on the king and his entourage that they had little autonomy. In fact, one of the strengths of the Buddhist clergy was that it provided the continuity that court life lacked. The situation in Burma was in marked contrast to the relatively independent Chinese bureaucratic structure built on an examination system that perpetuated government power through changes in political leadership and even dynasties. The lack of a bureaucracy was especially important in Burma because there was no recognized single line of succession to the throne. Thus cliques, centered around the king's brothers or his sons by many wives, fought for control of political power. Bureaucratic instability was the pattern. The elite structure at the top was subject to periodic and violent change. On annexation, Britain did not generally use indigenous leadership to assist in running the Burman parts of Burma, that is, Burma Proper. Rather, the new government staffed the bureaucracy with British at the higher levels and with Indians elsewhere.

Class structure in traditional Burma was pronounced, but it was fluid, at least for the Burman population. In addition to the central court and appointed officials, the populace was divided into *ahmudan*—a hereditary class of Burmans and some non-Burmans from central Burma who owed personal services to the court in lieu of taxes—and *athi,* who generally lived in Lower Burma and paid taxes, were drafted in wartime, and often were non-Burman. There were also indentured servants, or pagoda slaves, who were attached to maintain monuments. Villages were often divided by economic function. In spite of extensive Indian influence in many aspects of court life and philosophy, the caste system was never acceptable.

The position of traditional local elites in Burma was based on approval by and access to the court, however remote geographically. With such access came control over populations who farmed. Since land was plentiful, population relatively sparse and not bound to specific locales by ancestral or other immutable rites, physical mobility was possible and became evident. At the province level, the local official appointed by the court was called a *myoza* (literally, a "town eater"). His income depended on transmitting prescribed amounts of taxes to the court and pocketing the remainder. Excessive taxation, military service, or corvée labor requirements imposed from above, or greater economic opportunity elsewhere (for example, the opening of the Irrawaddy Delta rice lands in the nineteenth century) could cause migration from the locus of poverty or oppression. Great differentials in income did not seem widespread in the *myo* ("townships") among the bulk of the population.

The elite structure changed in the colonial era. Control of land was still important, but access to the British bureaucracy replaced the court as the route to power. Entrance into the bureaucracy at any but the lowest levels required a knowledge of English. Thus education became the prime requisite for secular social status, and an immense gulf developed between the English-speaking Burmese elite and the masses of the population. Education in the monastic school, the institution that had made Burma at that time the most literate nation east of the Suez with the exception of Japan, became irrelevant for this new need. Instead, secular status required attendance at English-language schools from the primary grades on up. Entrance to the university was the goal. The most prestigious avenue to success was, of course, attendance at a good university in England. Barring that, college in Burma was quite appropriate. Higher education was broadened in Burma in 1920 by fusing Rangoon College, a branch of the University of Calcutta, and Judson College, a missionary school. This led to more Burmese trained in the Western stream of education. The autonomous Burmese university, however, was still an elite institution, modeled on Oxford and Cambridge. A large portion of the student population was non-Burman, with a relatively high percentage of Christians. The aim of the students was to enter the Indian Civil Service and later the Burma Civil Service when it was formed after separation from India. They were the most elite of all bureaucratic organizations. Outside of these possibilities, any government position was desirable. As in South Asia, and indeed in most British colonies, the introduction of the British common law system for many functions created a demand for legal and paralegal skills. (Traditional Buddhist law was also maintained for specialized purposes.) Law became a favorite subject for those who wished to go into government and even for those who preferred to remain outside of it. Special attention was also given to some groups outside the Burman tradition. Kanbawza College was established in Taunggyi, capital of the Shan State, to educate the children of the Shan *sawbwa*s. It was an idyllic "public school" in the British tradition. Missionaries established many primary and secondary schools throughout the country. They taught in English.

Prestige, however, was not only a product of wealth or bureaucratic status that gave access to wealth. It was also a result of religious activity. Affluence allowed freedom of time, and time was essential for meditation and the attainment of higher status by rising through the innumerable series of rebirths, a result of personal *kan* ("karma"). If an individual had additional funds, he or she could enjoy the secular pleasures of this life and also become a *payataga* ("pagoda builder"), acquiring great merit, better rebirths with the promise of even more secular delights in the next – and better – reincarnation, and immediate social status as well.

World War II produced political ferment that was expressed in the pseudo-independent state sponsored by Japan and subsequently in the Anti-Fascist People's Freedom League that cooperated with the British. These disturbed conditions opened new channels of social mobility and widened existing ones for a broad segment of the population, especially in the wake of the Indian exodus. This mobility expanded further in the postwar and independence period.

There were four major channels of social mobility in Burman society: education, the army, politics and related activities such as labor unions, and the *sangha*. With a relatively weak clan and extended-family system, and without strong location-specific loyalties, advancement in Burman society became relatively easy after independence.

In the early period of independence, all education was free. It was common to find bright sons and, increasingly, daughters of peasant or worker families from all major ethnic groups attending the University of Rangoon and later Mandalay University or one of the provincial intermediate colleges. Although the children of economically advantaged families had greater access to better instruction through missionary or other private schools (a situation still prevalent through the mushrooming private tutoring schools), there was a remarkable diversity of socioeconomic backgrounds among the students. Since universities were free and dormitory facilities were often available, costs were not prohibitive. Students could also find inexpensive lodging in temples or in private homes. There was a clear and general understanding that a university degree was required for a government position and an appropriate marriage.

Yet, there was also a demand for technically trained individuals at all levels, especially those from the specialized technical secondary schools. A separate stream of technical education through the university level was designed to improve production in the state and private enterprises. It was not intended as an avenue to higher elite status, but it was used as such. Its participants considered technical education as a second-class system, a view reflecting both traditional British and Burman attitudes. Most students entered technical institutions only when they could not gain admittance to liberal arts programs at the universities; then they tried to transfer.

By the time of the military coup, graduates of the universities in both technical and liberal arts subjects had a difficult time finding jobs.

There was growing unemployment of educated people because the government could not absorb the numbers of graduates coming out of the universities, and opportunities in the private sector were limited. (In 1979, unemployment in Rangoon and Mandalay was over 14 percent and largely of educated individuals.) The only exception was at the artisan training level, where the poorest and lowest class sons went into technical schools at an early, post–primary age; they were immediately employed. The situation was not so acute for the unemployed as in some Western societies. Their families could support them, sometimes for years, until appropriate positions opened in government service. Even unemployed, the prestige of the university degree gave status to the student as a member of the elite.

The military was the second avenue of mobility. Before World War II, the army was the domain of the minority groups, a policy specifically designed by the British and based on an Indian model. It obviously kept the Burmans from having to deal harshly with other Burmans, for the military's primary role was to keep order in Burma Proper. Only one out of eight soldiers was Burman in 1940. This situation, of course, changed with independence and the Karen insurrection, which eliminated many of the large number of Karen who held certain key positions in the armed forces. Thereafter government policy encouraged large-scale Burman recruitment.

The military was an attractive career. It was open to all, and mobility was possible within it not only through inservice training courses, but also through the Defense Services Academy at Maymyo, which awarded University of Rangoon degrees. Top military leaders, united by their experience in the anti-British and then anti-Japanese struggles, formed a core that seemed initially to be less faction ridden than the elites in the upper levels of politics. There were, however, close ties between the military and the political leadership. They often came from related families, intermarried, and seemed motivated, at least initially, by many of the same forces. Both groups distrusted the elite civil service, which was too closely identified with the British.

Politics was the third avenue of mobility. Many individuals, some poorly educated, were early participants in the labor union movement and became active in the AFPFL. Some reached ministerial rank; others staffed the labor unions and the political parties of both the Left and the Center. Such a career required the least training, education, or discipline and was thus attractive to many.

The final avenue of social mobility was the *sangha*. Monastic education had been the hallmark of precolonial education. Most Burman sons and many daughters at that time attended the local school in the village or town monastery, where they were taught by monks and thus became literate. Monastic education continued through the colonial period. Even today, when secular primary education has virtually blanketed Burma, there are still many monastic schools. Those individuals who wanted to stay within the *sangha* for longer than the short time virtually required of every male in the Burman Buddhist environment could do so. Through careful study and adherence to the rules of the order, they could advance in education and finally graduate from the Pali University. Since mobility in and out of the *sangha* was accepted and easy (in marked contrast to life in the Catholic clergy), many students left the *sangha* at any point in their education and resumed lay life after having received a quite good, if traditional, education. Their role in the *sangha,* however temporary, gave them additional prestige in the Burman community. The political and nationalistic role of the monks in the pre- and post-colonial period prevented them from being shut out of the mainstream of political or intellectual life. In fact, the close association of socialism, nationalism, and Buddhism gave them a central role in the main tradition of Burman culture.

Gradually the military changed the role of education as an entrée into elite status. Student activism was not a new factor following the 1962 coup; it was evident from 1920 on and found greatest expression in the anticolonial struggles of the 1930s. Ne Win found it disquieting when he was prime minister under the caretaker government. When it occurred after the coup, he violently repressed it and tried to destroy its roots. Tertiary education was also producing an unemployed educated elite that could cause the regime even greater problems. To solve these issues, he reorganized education in 1964, stressing science for industrial development rather than liberal arts. He also turned the universities of Rangoon and Mandalay into a series of autonomous institutes and colleges that were designed to prevent cohesive student activism.

The plan did not work. Indeed, as economic problems increased, as the regime became more repressive, as the government could not employ the growing numbers of graduates, and as it discouraged the private sector, student activism and antimilitary demonstrations intensified. The universities were closed for perhaps one-fifth of the time between 1962 and 1976.

After the last major demonstrations in 1976, Ne Win ordered his second educational reform. If dividing the students into separate institutes, but keeping the bulk of them in Mandalay and Rangoon, did not work, then he determined to divide them even further by establishing a regional college system. The plan was also designed to assist in local economic development. Twenty two-year vocationally oriented junior colleges were established in each division and in every state except the Chin State. Students now spend two years near their homes attending the regional colleges, which have vocational emphases and charge modest fees. After this, they take examinations that may qualify them for one of the universities or institutes. If they do not pass or if they prefer, they remain in their regional college and take a third year in some technical skill. Many Burmese educators worry about a fall in standards of the last two years of undergraduate training because of poor preparation and wonder whether technical education will attract students and whether the skills taught are germane to local employment possibilities. These are unresolved issues. Technical education still seems to be a secondary avenue to prestige and elite status. Furthermore, half of the 32,000 students in the regional colleges in 1980 were still in those in Rangoon and Mandalay and thus were potentially politically active in areas where public demonstrations could spread. In addition, it may become more dangerous to the regime to have minority students study close to the locus of their ethnic loyalties than it would be to allow them to come to the melting pots of Mandalay and Rangoon.

The third educational reform that opened university degrees to more students was the organization of the correspondence course system in the latter 1970s. According to this system, working students can obtain a University of Rangoon degree by correspondence lessons, supplemented by a month of laboratory work, lectures, and examinations in residence at a university or regional college during normal vacation periods. Over 74,000 students in 1980 were enrolled in this program.

The effects of these reforms have been to broaden access to tertiary education, but also to lower the prestige of university degrees and graduates, to restrict entry into the top elite, and to heighten the status accruing to a University of Rangoon degree through attendance at the Defense Services Academy. In addition, because military education is free and normal university education requires tuition, there is greater mobility through the military, even though the numbers are much smaller.

Because the military has vastly expanded the system of primary education throughout the country—there were 1.8 million students in primary school in 1963 compared to 3.7 million in 1979—the role of and need for monastic education have correspondingly diminished, and its importance in mobility has now declined. Mobility was normally sought through education and politics as well. However, by diffusing education and lowering the graduates' status, by co-opting the political system through the formation of the BSPP and then controlling membership in it—stressing the military's role—the military has blocked these traditional avenues of advancement. In addition, peasant and labor organizations, as well as the BSPP, are virtual arms of the military. Thus, the new elites of Burma will likely be primarily recruited from the military, and insofar as they are civilian, determined by the military. This will probably cut off diversity of opinions and experience, forcing the nation into a uniform mold that may be disadvantageous for solving its problems. Social mobility is still widely evident in the military and seems to be encouraged, although there are charges that the children of the upper-level officers manage to have special privileges. Other avenues seem to have been restricted. This may be one of the most fundamental changes mandated by the military leadership. Its immediate effect will be to give the military a monopoly, not only of present power, but of leadership for the foreseeable future.

THE STATUS OF WOMEN

The Burman woman has had a high degree of freedom. This freedom, of which early European observers universally made note, was not a product of colonial concern, of missionary exhortations, or of Buddhism, but of the pre-Buddhist Burman society. As Scott wrote in *The Burman: His Life and Notions* (1910, 3rd. ed., p. 52), Burman women "have the further inducement that they enjoy a much freer and happier position than in any other European country, and in some respects are better off even than women in England." Written in 1883, these comments are still true. Burman women run the family finances and more importantly they control small retail trade, real estate, and are represented in large businesses. They are generally paid the male rate of pay for agricultural labor, and they staff the bureaucracy, although usually at lower levels than the males. Although they represent only 2 percent of the armed forces, they are 15 percent of the BSPP. Given the heavy military participation in the party, their percentage of the nonmilitary membership must be much higher among civilians than this low figure indicates.

Burman women have thorough equality of educational opportunity. Secular education having replaced monastic education, women make up half of the school population in Burma Proper and half of the regional college students. They are well represented as teachers from the primary to the university level. Half of the medical school graduates are women. Overall literacy rates for women in Burma Proper are 61 percent (35 percent in the states), compared to male rates of 83 percent, but they will rise. Among the non-Mon minority groups, female literacy is much less, although primary education has spread to those regions and the rate of female attendance is close to that of males.

Role differentiation in Burma caused the Burman woman, until recently, to assume certain occupations while eschewing others. It has been considered inappropriate for a Burman woman to have access to or

to touch males outside the family and for males to have similar relationships with women. Thus, as is common in many societies, birth atten-
dants were women. But as Western medicine was introduced, Burman
women became doctors, usually gynecologists, obstetricians, and pedia-
tricians. Today these patterns are changing as traditional taboos have
broken down. There is still a paucity of nurses in Burma compared to
doctors. In the past, Burman Buddhist women did not become nurses
and thus this profession was left to the Christian Karen, Chin, and
Kachin, who were not subject to the same taboos.

The Burman female brings her dowry with her in marriage, but retains and controls it, taking it with her if she divorces, which she is free
to do. Families are patrilineal, but residence after marriage, at least for a
period, is usually matrilocal. The female retains her name (there are no
surnames in Burma) and can inherit equally with her brothers. This is
true customarily and is legally recognized. She has equal rights under the
constitution and votes. Three articles of the Burmese constitution of 1974
specifically provide her with these rights.

In general, foreign observers have noted the dominance of the
female in the household. Her control of the finances enables her to be
generally quite autonomous. Many Burmans would also agree on the
dominant role of the female in marriage. The wife does, however, pay
public deference to the husband, although in reality the husband is controlled by and is dependent on the wife. An exception is in the case of
abortion, which does require the husband's consent; it is illegal, however, under normal circumstances. Although women may divorce easily,
and although divorce is not a difficult process, it is not common, perhaps
because the female's dowry is a stronge economic motive for continuing
the marriage.

The powerful role of the Burman woman may have roots in the
early preschool discipline and training as a result of the household responsibilities imposed on her by her family. In marked contrast, the
young male is not subject to discipline or responsibility until entry into
primary school. Thus her training may give the woman a sense of purpose and direction generally superior to that of males. Throughout her
life she retains her autonomy, controlling whom she will wed. There are
few arranged marriages. She is thoroughly economic in her outlook and
her acumen is reflected in her influence.

Although her actual status may be equal or even superior to that of
her husband, tradition requires that lip service be paid to the "superiority" of the male. The wife is supposed to respect her husband and not to
interfere with or diminish his glory, or *pon*. Since the source or seat of
this glory is in the male head, nothing, and especially no female or
feminine piece of clothing, is supposed to be above it. This custom may

reflect a later Buddhist influence. Women are often employed on construction sites carrying cement or building materials on their heads, while Burman males will not take such a job. Females also cannot enter nirvana without first being reincarnated as a male.

Some scholars claim that women have a higher status in more primitive or poorer societies because they work alongside the men and their work is required for family survival. The belief is that the status of women declines as a society becomes richer. Thus it became a mark of status to seclude a wife. In China, peasant women had a higher status among the peasantry than upper-class women had among the elite; peasant women had to work and did not have their feet bound.

The freedom of the Burman woman is shared with her Mon sisters. The high status of the Burman female may have influenced the status of some other minority women, such as the Karen or Shan, insofar as they had contact, but the low literacy rates among minority females indicate that they still lack considerable autonomy. In other Southeast Asian societies, such as Thailand, Indonesia, and the Philippines, women also have relatively high status. All have escaped the degradation of women to the west or north of them. There was no Indian suttee or Muslim purdah in Burma, nor was there Chinese foot binding. The autonomy of the Burman woman is one of the more attractive aspects of Burman culture.

BUDDHISM IN CONTEMPORARY BURMAN CULTURE

It is Buddhism that has moulded social Burman life and thought, and to the present day the ordinary Burman regards the terms Burman and Buddhist as practically equivalent and inseparable. The whole political and social life of Burma from the palace to the village centered around the Buddhist religion and monastic order (Furnivall 1957b, pp. 12–13).

For a Westerner to comprehend the overpowering dominance of Buddhism in Burman life and culture, it may be necessary to compare it to the position of the Catholic Church in medieval Europe, but assuming that all Catholic Europe was a single ethnic group. This does not imply that Buddhism is either medieval or rigid; rather that it is pervasive and the single most important force in everyone's life. It permeates the customs, the intellectual outlook, the philosophy, and indeed the political system of governance. In one form or another, it has existed in Burma since recorded history. Although Burman tradition has the Buddha visiting Burma, there is no evidence of Buddha or Buddhism's presence in Burma before the Vesali, Pyu, and Mon kingdoms.

The village monastery is the focus of village life. It traditionally pro-

vided the educational locus. One became literate through exposure to the
Buddhist canon, and thus literacy was inchoately associated with morality. Conversely, to be illiterate indicated a lack of moral standing.
Group activity, not only individual learning, focused on the monastery,
for the Burmans rarely engaged voluntarily in social group activities
beyond the family except as they related to Buddhism. The monk is not
only the respected leader of the community, he is often the healer,
counselor, consultant, teacher, and sometimes magician and alchemist.
Perhaps 2.5 to 3 percent of the adolescent and adult Buddhist males are
monks or novices at any one time, although half are in the *sangha* or associated with the monasteries for relatively short periods.

Life revolves around Buddhism. Each morning, in urban or rural
areas, the monks make the rounds of houses receiving donations of food
from the population. The monks themselves may or may not eat the
food, but the laity is not performing a kindly act in offering it; it is rather
the monk who provides a social and religious service by allowing the
populace to gain merit—to build up a karmic reserve that will allow
eventual rebirth at a more convenient or higher level of existence. The
major family nonsubsistence expenses are religious—offerings at pagodas, money spent for pilgrimages, for the ordination ceremony for a son
who will enter the monkhood as a novice for a short period, for the
ear-boring ceremony for a girl, and for the daily and festival feeding
of the monks and the presentation of gifts, such as robes, to them
on appropriate occasions. All require funds and may take from 10 to
25 percent of disposable income depending on wealth and status. All
of these activities provide both merit and social esteem, however. *Payataga* and *kyaungtaga* ("pagoda builder," "monastery builder") are terms
of the highest possible respect, indicating both that the deeds from previous incarnations allow the donor to accumulate both capital and merit
to engage in the building and that future incarnations will be still better.

Whether popular Buddhism in Burma is close to the ideals of the
classic Pali Buddhist canon is a subject of much dispute. Buddhism in
Burma is in any case inextricably linked with supernaturalism, magic,
and alchemy. The *nats*, or spirits, pervade Burman life. They are
everywhere and are always to be propitiated. The major national *nats*,
arranged in a pantheon of thirty-seven, are usually the spirits of living
beings who were "plucked green," who died violently before their time.
They must be appeased or they can cause mischief. Their home is in the
revered Shwezigon Pagoda near Pagan, and their placement in a Buddhist shrine was an attempt by Pagan rulers to amalgamate Buddhism
and pre-Buddhist religion, as they clearly represent a pre- or non-
Buddhist element of Burman society. So intricately have they become in-

terwoven into the Burman Buddhist fabric at the popular level that any attempted intellectual separation becomes a sterile form of textual criticism, unrelated to Burman reality. There are also village and household *nat*s, as well as a myriad of ghosts, who must also be placated. Alchemy, widely but quietly practiced, is related to Buddhism in that positive moral attributes are essential to its success. Astrology is also linked to Buddhism.

Buddhism is not only all-encompassing at the personal and village level, but it is equally critical at the national level and in all forms of intellectual endeavor. Because political organizations were banned in the early period of colonial rule, Buddhist organizations became the focus for early nationalist sentiment. British insensitivity to Buddhist customs exacerbated both nationalism and the importance of Buddhism. The political role of monks in the preindependence period has often been noted. After independence, monks campaigned for and against various political figures and parties. The parties used Buddhism as well. Monks also led progaganda campaigns against Communism at the behest of U Nu. The military used religion as well, publishing in the caretaker period *Dharma in Danger,* a booklet depicting the danger to Buddhism from the Left.

Buddhist thought traditionally integrated religion and social values. Pali terminology was used to translate socialist ideas into Burmese in the 1930s. Leaders such as U Nu specifically used Buddhist parables and folktales to explain to the public the welfare state they hoped to create. The intellectuals made efforts to demonstrate that Buddhism was modern, that a person could be scientific and Buddhist at the same time. There is no necessary dichotomy between traditional religious or animist beliefs and scientific thought or technological training, and there is no polarization between the religiously oriented U Nu and the secular Ne Win. Historically, Burma shifted and continues to shift today between militarily (secularly) oriented rulers and more religious ones without ideological trauma.

Traditionally the Burman monarch was defender of the faith; however, he was also sometimes regarded as an "embryo Buddha." The kings built monasteries, fed monks, and generally supported the religion. U Nu in 1954 convened the Sixth Great Buddhist Synod (there had only been five synods since the time of the Buddha) to clarify and correct textual errors. By so doing, he was consciously acting in the tradition of the Burmese kings, specifically in the tradition of King Mindon (1853–1878), who convened the fifth synod. In both cases, the convening of the synod was an effort to establish the legitimacy of a new regime and its central figure. In 1980 when Ne Win convened the all *sangha* meeting, he too was acting in this great tradition. In a tradition continuous in Burma since Pagan, U Nu completed the World Peace Pagoda in Rangoon in 1952. Ne

Win, in the same manner, ordered the construction of a pagoda in 1980. The king's role in Buddhism also provided legitimacy. It is also important to note that both the traditional and modern ruler's emphasis on Buddhism was not only part of the process of legitimization and of establishing political appeal, but it was as well an attempt to control the independent Buddhist *sangha* and bring it under the authority of the state.

In spite of the myriad, multicolored, and diversely motivated rebellions that have plagued Burma since independence, the only sustained efforts that have emanated from the Burman population, in contrast to those of the minorities, have come from the left wing. It is significant that each of these rebellions has been on the fringes of society, and in some cases leadership was significantly non-Burman. These revolts have had relatively little impact on the bulk of the Burman population. In spite of economic provocation, the vast majority of Burmans—especially those in rural areas, who may be more traditional or who have access to sufficient food—has been quiescent.

Why has this been so? Is there something about the Burman Buddhist ethic that raises the level of political tolerance, allowing rulers to run their course without overt expressions of protest from the people? Does Buddhism, with its teaching that position in life is determined by past karmic rewards, tend to allow a greater degree of political license on the part of rulers? The population knows that an evil ruler will suffer retribution, at the philosophical level in a less desirable incarnation, at the popular level in one of the many Buddhist hells. Peasant rebellions have been relatively rare in Burma, and those that have developed have had a foreign focus or were attempts to establish a new kingdom or both. Few seemed economically oriented or motivated against a political regime for excesses that it committed (as opposed to personal rivalries among opposed leaders). Urban demonstrations have been more common, but aside from those involving students, they had economic stimuli. Lack of data prevents an answer to the question of political tolerance, but the relative underpopulation of the rural areas, their isolation intellectually and geographically, physical mobility, the lack of starvation—together with some unknown degree of Buddhist tolerance—may be responsible. The case for Buddhist political tolerance in Burma has often been asserted, but never proven.

In traditional Burma, productive private investment was not possible, for the king controlled all foreign trade and a considerable amount of the country's production and internal trade as well. Insofar as economic expansion occurred, it was state controlled. Thus the modern socialist state may be considered both as an effort to create a secular modernization program and also as a reversion to traditional monarchical practices. In the colonial period, European, Indian, and Chinese monopolies of credit and capital gave these groups access to the modern sector of the economy, which the Burmans did not understand for long periods. This left the Burmans essentially excluded from the considerable growth that developed in colonial Burma, a classic economic model of an economy that produced and partially processed its own raw materials.

Burman Buddhist society does encourage religious donations of all sorts, a rational investment for those who participate, in spite of the exhortations of Western economists. Instead of being subject to the economic and political vagaries of investment, nationalization, taxation, bribery, or dacoity, the building of religious merit through religious use of surplus capital is a sound investment for the future. Not only does a person gain religious capital in the cosmic bank, but by such donations he or she assures a better existence next time in which to enjoy better the secular pleasures of the material world. Yet Burman Buddhist society offers many advantages that could stimulate economic growth. These include the high status and productive employment of women, a fluid class structure, interest in education, and a highly literate population. The downgrading of the private sector that started with independence and reached its peak under the military prior to 1972 acted as a spur to non-productive investment. With nationalization of industry and land, low rice prices, the inability to have the right to inherit land, and forced procurement of paddy and other crops, there were fewer opportunities to create surpluses. Any surpluses that were accumulated could not be invested productively. Under military policy, the only credible choices centered around religious giving, always safe and prestigious, or investment in the nonproductive but highly lucrative smuggling or illegal internal trade, where profits were immediate and extensive, if religious rewards were not. If the military's goals were to discourage individual initiative in economic growth and to encourage the people to use surpluses for religious giving, they could hardly have devised a better policy. Traditionally, economic development may have been retarded by Buddhist religious donations, but today the barrier to development lies more in government policy than in religious doctrine.

Even in the traditional period, however, religious building should not be considered solely an economic drain on the state. The construction of pagodas did spur subsidiary employment, including crafts and services, and increase the demand for agricultural products, and thus helped encourage production. The increased wealth of the state (that is, of the king) led to the cyclical rise and decline of Buddhist institutional power. As wealth accumulated, more pagodas were built, and the *sangha,* in contrast to the rules of the order, became rich. The king then was forced to purify the *sangha* to get land and people back into the tax base and equally to gain more merit, because a purified *sangha* to which offerings were made would yield a higher rate of meritorious return than donations to a corrupt one. Once the *sangha* was purified, more donations would flow in, and thus the *sangha* would once again become rich and the economic base of the state would retract, bringing on another purification rite. Colonial policy cut the cycle.

Today, Burma has ostensibly retreated from Buddhism as the military has created a secular state. The 1961 act making Buddhism the state religion has, in effect, been overthrown. The military dissolved the Buddha Sasana Council in April 1962 and repealed the Pali University Act in 1965. It attempted to assert its dominance and register all Buddhist organizations in April 1965, although the later edict was rescinded after monastic demonstrations. The 1974 constitution omits references to Buddhism. Yet U Nu is back in Burma under government auspices working on Buddhist matters, and the military is sponsoring the construction of a major pagoda. When Ne Win in effect disestablished *nat* worship, he did so in the name of purifying Buddhism. Thus, the dichotomy between the military secular ruler and state under Ne Win and the religiously oriented one under U Nu cannot be maintained. It was not true in Burmese history, and it is equally not true today.

THE ARTS AND INTELLECTUALS

In much the same manner that Burman Buddhist values permeated the nationalist movement, traditionally education, literature, dance, and the plastic arts were encouraged in the service of Buddhism. Monastic education was important, but with the exception of some drama and poetry, literature was essentially religious, the retelling of the numerous *jataka* tales of the Buddha's previous existences. Plays, dances, puppetry, painting, and sculpture all derived their inspiration and their patrons from the same source.

The British period transformed some of the arts. Wood carving, the great genius and heart of Burman creativity as the remains from the great monasteries from the Burman kingdoms testify, fell into disarray without royal patronage. Western-style painting was introduced, but its influence was limited to a few urban centers and it fell under the baneful domination of tepid British landscape and watercolor schools. Drama and dance, however, the form of village and mass entertainment, flourished. Burmese dance received new vigor with the introduction of Thai dancers and art forms following the Burmese conquest of Ayuthia in 1767. Under the impetus of new technology, modern elements, such as electric stage lighting, costumes of synthetic fibric, and other innovations, not all of which were progress, were introduced, but the tradition continued and the demand for these arts never ceased. The novel and

Western-style drama found a ready audience. There was no split among the writers and intellectuals and the political process. Both politicians and monks wrote literature. U Nu wrote several plays in Western style. These books, and most other writings except poetry, were directed toward political and social problems.

Under democratic governments, the arts were encouraged. The government established the Burma Translation Society to spread ideas from abroad as well as those home grown. Works for the newly literate were published, as well as those designed to improve rural life. Prizes were awarded for the best books in all catagories of literature. Standardized new Burmese terms were coined for imported and modern concepts, and textbooks were published using these terms. Many novels were printed, the most famous of which were topical in content. Among the most influential authors was the outspoken Thein Pe Myint, who, starting in the 1930s, was noted for his leftist and iconoclastic views.

Newspapers were a product of foreign influence. The first, in English, started in British Burma in 1836, and the first Burmese paper appeared in the Arakan in 1873. Other Burmese papers followed in Rangoon in 1873 and in Mandalay in 1874. At independence, there were thirty-nine papers published in Burma, including five in Chinese, two in Hindi, one each in Urdu, Tamil, Telegu, and Gujarati.

After the military coup of 1962, the government restricted the press and gradually nationalized it. In September 1962, the 1962 Printers and Publishers Act was passed, revoking all previous publishing laws dating back to 1876. It was the most restrictive in Burmese history, licensing the presses for only one year at a time. A Press Registration Board and a Press Scrutiny Agency were created. By 1963, a Burmese news agency, set up by government, controlled all foreign news agencies, and the same year the Revolutionary Council founded the *Working People's Daily*, the official government organ. It was first printed in Burmese and then a year later in English as well. By 1966, the press had been nationalized, along with all foreign language publishing except in English. There are now two government controlled English-language dailies in Burma. Both print essentially the same news. By 1975, the BSPP had issued new guidelines for publishing. All works including novels and magazines had to promote socialism—the national ideology—contribute to national unity, promote the national culture, and spread progressive ideas from all nations. Conversely, any publication that tended to destroy or ridicule these ideas, or was obscene or libelous, was banned. Criticism was allowed, but only when it was constructive and did not question the state-proclaimed goals.

Newspapers and other printed media were widely circulated in urban areas, yet circulation (if not readership) of the ten leading dailies was only 212,000 in 1970, a very small number considering the population of the four or five major cities. Distribution problems limited newspaper influence in rural areas. Newspapers were read by the elite and the university and bureaucratic communities. They had little influence on the masses. Radios had a greater effect. There were 388,000 registered in 1968, but probably many more had been smuggled in and were uncounted. Since about 6 percent of villages have electricity, the transistor opened communications in Burma as no other single innovation could. Broadcasting is controlled by the government. Most of it is in Burmese, although there is a half hour per day in Kachin, Chin, Shan, Arakanese, Kayah, Mon, and Sgaw and Pwo Karen dialects. The first television station was introduced into Burma in 1980, with the assistance of the Japanese. The Burmese film industry and imported films are rigidly controlled. The quality of locally produced, and even locally shown imported films, is low. There are over 450 movie theaters throughout the country.

The most popular form of entertainment is still the *pwe*, the all-night spectacle that combines song, dance, and drama. It adds humor, sparkle, and excitement to an otherwise humdrum existence. Although the military has on occasion attempted to control even this form of amusement, here satire can and does exist. The glitter of the stage and the spoofs of the clowns are combined with religious teachings and history. The popularity of this form of drama and vaudeville has kept alive the traditions of dance and music, both of which are taught at government institutions.

Soon after the coup, the military began to hold a series of meetings to explain to intellectuals, writers, and journalists the goals of the state, attempting to co-opt their services for national ends. In 1965, an Organization Committee for the Federation of Literary Workers was formed, but the ideological differences between the writers and the government prevented an organization from developing at that time. Intellectuals complained about the jailing of newspapermen and journalists. The issue was not resolved until 1980 when the government finally succeeded in organizing a federation of writers. Chapters now exist in 77 townships with an additional 52 with organizing committees. Membership includes 2,377 writers and 768 journalists. It is another form of political control under party domination.

The position of the intellectual qua intellectual in Burmese society has never been strong compared to China and Japan, for example. University professors have considerable prestige, but perhaps it is more linked to their status as senior civil servants than to that of professor, although the term *saya* ("teacher") is one of great respect because it was once associated with the role of the monk as teacher. The monk is known as *sayadaw* ("honored teacher").

The military has allowed criticism only insofar as the goals of the state were not questioned. Performance may be criticized, but not ideology. Contemporary intellectual and artistic creativity, with the exception of dance and music, is stifled. The military has attempted to provide literary awards to those writers who further the political and economic goals of the state. It is significant that many prizes each year are not awarded because the military has not been able to channel intellectual activities as it had planned. With a few notable exceptions, the sterility of the intellectual endeavors made public do little justice to the people who have produced one of the great cultural traditions in Southeast Asia.

THE CONTINUITY OF BURMAN CULTURE

U Nu remarked soon after the formation of the Union of Burma, "We lost our independence without losing our self-respect; we clung to our culture and our traditions and these we now hold to cherish and to develop in accordance with the genius of our people." (Trager 1966, p. 91). The Burmans have tenaciously tried to retain their culture, as U Nu stated. It has been, as we have seen, a conscious policy. Yet unconsciously the Burmans have maintained many of their traditions and incorporated traditional attitudes in many of their new institutions. For example, political and administrative systems that were formed to overturn past practices may have drawn on and reinforced traditional views. This is not surprising in spite of the colonial experience. British influence was powerful at the national level and reached down to the village, but it was of relatively short duration in central Burma where Burman values had their roots. Aside from the disestablishment of Buddhism, the British did little directly to interfere with Burman customs. Since the Buddhist structure in the monarchical period was a loose one, even this had a marginal affect, although to the Burmans it was the single greatest cause for concern after the loss of independence. Thus Buddhism became associated with nationalism, and the separation of church and state simply increased the importance of Buddhism's role and the intensity of the Burman identification with it.

As we have seen, both U Nu, as a consciously devout Buddhist leader, and Ne Win, as an essentially secular figure, used Buddhism for political and personal ends, continuing the tradition of the Burman kings. They perhaps unconsciously used the traditional symbols, including those of Buddhism, as part of their socialist programs. U Nu did this in formulating and illustrating the Pyidawtha welfare state, and Ne

Win did it in publishing *The System of Correlation of Man and His Environment*. It is significant that Ba Maw, U Saw, and U Nu all engaged in the fertility rite of ritual plowing, as did the Burman monarchs, to ensure successful crops. Socialism has become almost a millennial concept, the attainment of which has been pushed into the future, now to 1994. It is similar to the millennial Buddhist attitudes that permeate Burman Buddhist thinking.

The pattern extends beyond Buddhism and includes supernatural elements indigenous to the Burmans. Under U Nu, the government could order the construction of tens of thousands of sand pagodas to ward off national disaster. Nowhere is the evidence more complete, however, than in the officially sponsored reinterpretation and magnification of the role of Aung San. He was a great leader, the father of Burmese independence. Under officially sponsored stimuli, he has also become in popular eyes almost a *nat*. His violent death is an illustration of an essential element of *nat* culture, and his omnipresent picture taken in London in a greatcoat gives him an otherwordly aura in the tropics. It hangs in every government office and in many homes. His writings are quoted, sometimes out of context, to justify present policy. His appeal internationally was through his modern speeches, but his acceptance among the peasantry is based on his more traditionally oriented writings. His death is remembered in impressive national ceremonies annually. In the popular press he has even been mentioned as the reincarnation of King Alaungpaya, a strong monarch who unified Burma. Ne Win, as Aung San's close associate, has clearly gained in prestige as a result.

Just as politics in the past was highly personalized, and as political authority was regarded as an extension of personal *awza* ("power"), so today political life is essentially a continuation of traditional political authority systems, in spite of the elaborate political structure of a Pyithu Hluttaw and the ever-present Burma Socialist Programme party. As knowledge was power traditionally, so today the government attempts to control access to information and restricts its dissemination. Even the new ritual of succession under the Pyithu Hluttaw is remarkably similar to the pattern of choosing a new king under the traditional Hluttaw. The elimination of the administrative district, a British innovation in Burma, and the reversion to the township, or *myo*, evokes a past administrative pattern. The military's opening of an institute for Ayurvedic medicine, a traditional medicine based on very early Indian medical ideas, is a sign of this revival of traditions. Is it happenstance that Ne Win eventually married a granddaughter of the last reigning Burman monarch, King Thibaw? It was a traditional practice both in Burma and in other Southeast Asian nations for new kings to marry the daughters of former monarchs. That Ne Win's son married into the family of the Kengtung *sawbwa* is also part of Burman historical patterns.

Much as the monarchy created a monopoly on economic power, so today the state has developed a system that continues that tradition. Although data are lacking, and in spite of overwhelming propaganda campaigns, the populace probably still regards government as one of the five evils, as a Burmese proverb states. Traditionally, government was viewed as inherently evil and personalized. The king was a despot. Government was pervasive, influencing religion, but also social life and customs. It was unpredictable and not the concern of the people. Similar attitudes, both on the part of government and the governed, probably exist today. The military may appear to be revolutionary, but its actions could be interpreted as conservative in its preservation of Burman culture and in its evocation of an idealized past. If a modern bureaucracy has been created, it still functions like a traditional entourage, denying the government the lower-level autonomous decision-making ability that it has in principle espoused. It is not surprising that when the great earthquake occurred at Pagan in July 1975, some felt that it portended the collapse of the government.

The military has attempted positively to use the nationalist and Buddhist tradition to generate popular enthusiasm in other ways. In June 1980, the government established a new series of prizes and awards to honor those involved in the nationalist struggle. These included individuals who were active in the General Council of Buddhist Associations, the Saya San Rebellion, the student union and strikes, and the Thirty Comrades. Special attention was also given to the sixtieth anniversary of National Day, in commemoration of the anticolonial student strike of December 2, 1920. Union Day annually celebrates the signing of the Panglong Agreement in 1947.

Too much emphasis can be placed on cultural continuity; yet the evidence points to the strength of the Burman tradition and to the conscious and unconscious use of it in creating a new state. The tragedy is that this great tradition is considered the only major heritage worth evoking, although the more complex Burmese past contains many more traditions that might also have contributed to a more harmonious Burmese future.

7

The Search for
the Golden Land

Over 1,800 years ago in the West, the distant and vague area of the world that today is called peninsular Southeast Asia was known as *suvannaphumi,* or *chryse* (the "golden land"). Thus named by the Alexandrine Claudius Ptolomy in A.D. 165, this appellation connoted a region wealthy not only in gold but in other resources as well. The area was aptly named.

To many, Burma has been the golden land. The Burmese have felt singularly comfortable there. Until the coup of 1962, they rarely emigrated. They preferred their own land to any other. The Western traveler sometimes unconsciously felt the appropriateness of this name, exemplified in the gilded wonder of the Shwedagon Pagoda rising as high as Saint Paul's cathedral in London and symbolizing both the faith and the literal embodiment of *chryse.* The Indian laborer felt it metaphorically, as he migrated to Rangoon to escape the bleak poverty of Calcutta or Madras. The European and Chinese businessmen felt it, thinking of the rich rice lands of the Irrawaddy Delta, the vast teak forests, and the ruby and jade mines of the north. Even the contemporary academician responds similarly to the cultures of Burma, both attractive and underdocumented.

The potential of Burma is still there, largely unfulfilled. Still underpopulated compared to its neighbors and with its potentially arable land, its resources have been only marginally tapped. Rice production as well as yields of other crops could be doubled. Burma's mineral resources are underutilized and in some cases not fully explored. Its offshore wealth in fisheries, minerals, and potentially oil have just begun to be exploited in the past few years, although oil is still to be found. What are the prospects for this diverse and complex land, the largest in peninsular Southeast Asia?

THE ROAD TOWARD SOCIALISM

The integral relationship between socialism and nationalism, thus between socialism and political legitimacy, will continue to propel the ruling groups of Burma along a socialist track. Obeisance to this doctrinally required goal may sometimes conflict with reality, as it did first in 1955 and then again in 1971. Even when pragmatism wins and socialist policies must be curtailed so that less doctrinaire economic measures may right a listing economic ship of state, the reaffirmation of socialist principles serves to remind the populace of the legitimacy of the egalitarian quest. The culmination of political and economic planning—achieving an industrialized socialist state—has been set back to 1994. As targets become more elusive, the goal of a secular nirvana may have to be pushed still further into the future, recalling the interminably distant goals of some of the Burmese Buddhist sects.

Burma's economic reforms, announced in 1972 and implemented with some hesitation, have turned around a stagnant economy, transforming a deteriorating economic picture at home and a disastrous export performance into internationally respectable growth rates. Good weather has been an important factor in attaining the highest rice yields in Burmese history, but improved seed, greater use of fertilizer, and better monitoring have also been critical. The anomaly is that despite improved performance, exports have never approached the prewar levels. Yet agricultural prospects appear fair and could even be markedly improved if price and marketing incentives were offered to the Burmese farmer.

Burma's industrial expansion continues, but the emphasis has shifted somewhat to agro-based industries, and this is supportive of the new investment priority in agriculture and related fields. The industrialization goal remains but is couched in political platitudes with no realistic schedule. As the military has entrenched itself in power, it has felt a diminishing need to create a new Burmese proletariat that would contribute to the socialist revolution, perhaps one goal of the early military industrialization program.

The economic reforms, including material incentives, better tax policies, and even a grudging admission that the private sector could contribute to economic growth, have had a salutary effect on the economy. However, the new growth was financed by large-scale investment that had to come from abroad. Annual levels of foreign assistance rose over twenty times from 1971 to 1980. Most development investment is now foreign financed. The administrative and absorptive capacities of the government and its planning mechanism are now strained. As Burma becomes more dependent on bilateral and multilateral assistance, dangers of a resurgence of nationalism and xenophobia are ever present. Ironically, the attainment of Burma's socialist goals is increasingly dependent on foreign capitalist economies and their contributions to the mulitnational banks.

The major private sector in Burma is still agriculture. If the Burmese government were to succumb to its own ideological pressures and attempt to diminish drastically the role of the private sector to meet publicly announced targets, it would have to adopt one of two policies: the forced collectivization of land or the forced establishment of agricultural cooperatives. The state could easily make either move by proclamation, since title to all land is vested in the state. Neither policy would, however, increase production or improve equity and instead might prompt peasant unrest if living standards did not improve. The administrative machinery of the state is stretched thin already, and further state involvement may not prove effective.

The other hallmark of the Burmese socialist state is economic and social egalitarianism. It was only in 1976, after the economic reforms approved in 1972 began to be felt, that the Burmese standard of living finally reached the prewar level. In addition, Burma has less maldistribution of income among economic classes than most non-Communist societies. The highest 20 percent of the population controls 40 percent of the national income, whereas the lowest 20 percent has 8 percent. Land reform has been effective. The average farm size is 5.4 acres, and 86.8 percent of all farms are under 10 acres. Foreign landlords are gone; yet the state could be as unsympathetic a landlord as any Chettyar. The Burmese government's contribution to its own development plans is essentially financed by an indirect tax on the farmer through low paddy prices and an onerous procurement requirement.

No matter how rigid and dictatorial the government's rice pricing and procurement policies may be, the state has pushed forward the provision of social services. Although of low overall financial priority, the government has made important advances in education and health. Access to education has been vastly increased throughout the whole society, and budgets have risen to reflect this; yet there has been a per capita disinvestment in education in constant prices as the population has increased and inflation has risen. A concerted effort by the state has expanded health services to rural areas through both doctors and paramedics. Although woefully inadequate, and still of low fiscal priority, Burma's stress on preventive health and rural services is a model for many developing countries. The reality of the appropriation process in Burma, however, still places emphasis on curative services and undercuts the government's own health planning.

The economic flexibility evidenced through the reforms is further demonstrated in the tacit tolerance of the vast and pervasive black market and smuggling operations that seem to reach even quite remote regions of the nation. Capitalism, if not overtly alive and well, flourishes under studied government neglect. This economic flexibility, evidenced informally in the illegal trade and formally through the reforms of 1972, has no counterpart in the political sphere. Burma is governed by a rigid, single-party dictatorial political system under the constitution of 1974, which allows no essential divergence from the party line. The party in turn is firmly in the hands of the military. With essentially token representation in the highest levels of the decision-making process from the minorities, the military-cum-party superstructure is controlled by the Burman majority.

As the reforms of 1972 are felt, as conditions improve, it will be difficult for any regime to return to the more doctrinaire policies of the first decade of military rule. Vested interests have developed supportive of these changes. Yet it is also unlikely that there will be a shift from the socialist path that has proven to be so important psychologically to the Burmese. The attainment of Burma's own socialist objectives and the realization of its economic potential may be undercut by the rigidity of the party structure and the concomitant need for party orthodoxy. Burma's potential is far from realization, but there has been impressive progress, although it has been uneven.

BURMAN VERSUS BURMESE

If the Union of Burma under civilian leadership was an imperfect ideal, neither completely satisfying the majority Burman population nor meeting the demands of many of the minorities, then the Union of the Socialist Republic under Ne Win is a fiction. The nation is now symmetrical under the 1974 constitution, with seven divisions representing the Burman majority and seven states representing the minorities. Yet these bureaucratic entities, in spite of the election of their own representatives to the Pyithu Hluttaw and to their people's councils, have little internal power. The policies of the nation are determined through a military-dominated coterie of party officials at the center. There is less authority today at the periphery than there was under the civilian governments.

The unitary state of the 1974 constitution thus represents a retreat from even the modest autonomy of the U Nu era. The rigidity of the political structure, together with continued military domination, bodes ill for future amicable relations among ethnic groups. If the institutionalization of power in the hands of the Burmans works against minority

equality, so too does the identification of the mainstream of Burmese culture with the Burman culture. In spite of cosmetic attention to minority
cultures, the goals of the state have focused on political, economic, and
cultural integration and assimilation. If foreign imperialists were insensitive to Burman aspirations and problems during the colonial period,
the Burmans themselves have revealed this same insensitivity toward
the minorities. As possessors of what they regard a higher culture than
that of many of the tribes, and as traditional unifiers and bearers of
power within the state, they have tended to look down on the minorities.
Insofar as minorities adopted Christianity to any appreciable degree,
they have equated the interests of these minorities with those of Christian powers, thus further politicizing antagonisms.

From the Burman vantage point, the secession of minority states,
the balkanization of Burma, would spell political and economic disaster.
It would be ideologically unacceptable. The Burman monarchs were su-
zerains over the minority groups at the periphery, however little real
authority they may have exercised. Independence from colonial rule was
won by the Burmans. Burma's dissolution into several states would lead
to great power efforts to subvert their fragile independence and to use
them for other purposes. Economically, the states would have little
means to support themselves, except for those with access to the sea,
even though the minority regions contain much of the wealth of Burma.
No government at the center would willingly allow such resources to
pass from its control.

The minorities see reality differently. They feel subjugated politically, economically, and culturally to an insensitive majority that is
primarily concerned with its own identity. That identity is centered on a
social system and a religious heritage that are not always, or even often,
shared with the minorities. The Karen remember the massacres in the
delta during World War II and the bloody early days of the insurrection;
the Shan *sawbwas*, the loss of their rights; the Shan peoples, the arrogance of the Burma army; the Kachin, the ceding of some of their villages to China under the border settlement of 1960; and the Arakanese,
the flight of 200,000 Muslims to Bangladesh out of fear for the Burmese
military. There are much historical and emotional impedimenta to overcome.

The majority-minority tensions are not simply a result of history,
ethnicity, or religion. They have become more complicated by the interplay of externally generated politics and economics. The illegal smuggling trade between Burma and Thailand has given the Karen and Shan
insurgents in the border regions a secure economic base from which to
defy Rangoon. By taxing shipments in transit through their areas and by
producing teak and minerals for export, the insurgents have developed

sophisticated administrations that are self-perpetuating. In a sense, because of this trade and the unfulfilled hope of foreign support, they have been more outward looking than has the Burmese government for many years under the military. In addition, the opium trade in the Shan and Kachin states provides funds for the military resupply of a variety of factionally oriented independent armies. Even increased autonomy or independence would be unlikely to wipe out such a lucrative trade. The sporadic alignment of one or another of the ethnic rebellions with the Burma Communist party, the major base of which lies astride the Burma-China border in the remote trans-Salween region of the northern Shan State, adds a major element of uncertainty to an already murky picture.

Yet the central government has neither the manpower nor the military mobility to do more than simply contain these rebellions and prevent them from threatening the regime. Even this effort, together with the forces needed to counter the Burma Communist party troops and those required to ensure domestic tranquility in Burma Proper, forces the government to allocate over one-third of its annual budget to defense expenditures, leaving little for domestic development programs. Thus Burman-Burmese tension impedes the attainment of Burma's own development goals.

The prognosis is thus for continuing interethnic tension, which can only be alleviated by a breadth of vision, first on the part of the Burman leadership and then on that of the minorities. Such leadership seems a long way off and may require both a new locus of power at the center and a new generation on the periphery.

FOREIGN AFFAIRS

On independence, Burma declined membership in the British Commonwealth. The pattern of neutrality in the great power struggles was set within two years after independence and has been a continuing policy of each regime. Burma voted to brand North Korea as an aggressor in the Korean War and approved the sending of troops to Korea under UN auspices, but it voted against naming China as an aggressor in 1950. Burma voted against the Russian invasion of Hungary. It was in favor of North Vietnam during the latter period of the Vietnam war. This broad characterization of Burmese foreign policy does not do justice to the complexity of the Burmese position, which, within the overall neutralist position, has shifted markedly in response to both internal and external stimuli.

China has had an overpowering influence on Burma. If Burma has been neutral, it has been so in a China context, continuously assuring, insofar as possible, that relations with Peking were appropriate. Burma was the first non-Communist nation to recognize the People's Republic of China. The nationalist Kuomintang retreat into Burma and the arming and supply of those troops by Taiwan and the United States prompted Burma to close, for the first time, the U.S. aid program to Rangoon in 1953. Burma's friendly relations with Peking continued through the era of Bandung, with frequent exchanges of high-level visits between the two. The signing of the border agreement between China and Burma in 1960 was an important step for both nations. It enhanced the prestige of Ne Win, then head of the caretaker government, and allowed China to demonstrate to the world, at little cost to itself, that it had no geographical claims on its southern neighbors at a time when the Sino-Indian war was still fresh.

In 1961, China assisted Burma with a major $84 million aid program. It was abruptly suspended in 1967, when the anti-Chinese riots, precipitated by efforts to import the Cultural Revolution into Burma, led to a break in diplomatic relations. Those riots shifted the focus of urban discontent away from the military and onto a foreign power. In spite of the resulting tension between the two governments, Ne Win may have been pleased, for without an external enemy, unrest could easily have centered on him. There is little evidence prior to 1968 that the Chinese supplied any major assistance to the BCP, although after that date support seemed forthcoming.

The retreat into isolation following the coup of 1962 seemed to many a violation of Burmese neutrality, for if Burma remained nonaligned, it was nonaligned along a very leftish road. Burma's closure of World Bank activities seemed an unnecessary act, but it was perhaps prompted by an antipathy to having foreigners observe closely the Burmese economy. The result was that Burma relied on Japanese assistance throughout the period of its isolation, with some help from China until the break in relations in 1967.

Three factors have improved Burma's relations with the West, especially the United States. First, the end of the Vietnam war finally removed a major impediment to better relations between the two countries. Second, the improved relations between the United States and China were critical in the Burmese resumption of economic relationships with the United States and in the provision of U.S. assistance for antinarcotics activities in Burma. Third, the necessary shift to more liberal economic policies internally and the need to seek outside foreign assistance for that program all worked to bring Burma back into world economic relationships. Burma's withdrawal from the nonaligned states conference in Havana in the summer of 1979 signaled to the world that Burma would not let its important relations with Peking be jeopardized by what it regarded as the misuse of that meeting for Russian purposes in the Sino-Soviet split.

Burma will continue to be neutral. Its foreign policy is likely to be guided by concern about China and the need for external economic assistance.

THE OUTLOOK FOR BURMA

Burma's future is in part captive of its past and in part dependent on the wisdom of its leadership, present and future. If Burma has unconsciously attempted to provide a Burman identity solution to a Burmese identity problem, its government has done the same by institutionalizing a Burman unitary solution to the problem of Burmese diversity. This will continue to undercut Burmese stability, development, and growth, as well as the attainment of its social goals.

The immediate future of Burma will depend on the results of the transition to new leadership. The new process has half begun. In August 1981, President Ne Win, immediately after his reelection as chairman of the BSPP, announced his planned resignation as president of the Socialist Republic of the Union of Burma following the inauguration of the new Pyithu Hluttaw in November 1981. Although he wished to retire completely, he indicated his willingness to retain the party chairmanship, in effect maintaining his control over the political process and the choice of his successor. In August, he dropped San Yu from the party Central Committee, in obvious preparation for the presidency. In November, the Council of State formally elected San Yu the new president.

After ruling by decree for twelve years and remaining in power for almost two decades, Ne Win has institutionalized a method for change in the political leadership. In fact, he has manipulated the choice and guaranteed the result. He can do so as long as he is available and maintains interest in the process. The future is uncertain.

The new process ensures the means of selection, but it cannot produce a leader who can command the respect that Ne Win has garnered. No system can. Ne Win may be sui generis. No other leader in Burma has had such a long and illustrious career, an association with the independence movement, and the aura of having taken the mantle of Aung San, father of independent Burma. In addition, because of Ne Win's long leadership, no other figure has solely collected debts of gratitude from so many for their political advancement. Ne Win's successor will be hard pressed to maintain power without these credentials.

The longer-range future is less clear than the immediate. President San Yu is in titular command, but all eyes remain on Ne Win. What, then, of the period following four years of San Yu? He may, of course, retain control or try to do so, as most Burmese leaders have. But if not San Yu, what leader or leaders will emerge in the post–Ne Win period? U Nu is back in Burma under the amnesty of the summer of 1980 and is engaged in religious work, long his special and overriding interest. Although noted as holding strong views that he was the last legitimate leader of Burma, U Nu seems uninterested and even now may be too elderly to take on the onerous task of national leadership, nor is it likely that high military authorities would allow him to do so. Other civilian politicians from previous governments seem unacceptable as well, no matter how strongly socialist they may have been.

Most likely, leadership will come from the military. Having controlled, co-opted, or closed other avenues of mobility, the real and potential sources of power rest in their hands. Ne Win, however, by virtue of his role since independence, when he was first deputy commander of the armed forces and then commander in 1949, has risen above cliques and factions. Burmese political life has been generally characterized more by the development of circles of personal loyalties that encourages entourages and factionalism than by ideological or philosophical differences. The Burma army shows no signs that it alone is impervious to such stress. Thus, factionalism within the military may play an important future role.

Would a military-cum-party junta that would share power be a solution to the problem of Burmese leadership? Such a compromise might temporarily satisfy contending leaders, of whom there may be a number, but it would be unlikely to last except in the face of an overriding threat to national survival. It is possible that intensified minority revolts and agitation, or an expanded drive by the Burma Communist party, during such a transition might be viewed as such a threat, but in any event this solution would be unlikely to endure.

In the short run, changes in economic policy are likely to depend on the stability of the political leadership. The direct effects of economic reform on the population will be felt slowly. Although those who wish to see the reforms contined will be influential, those in government who want continued liberalization may not have popular support until the reforms make a direct and positive impact on the population's wellbeing. Thus, the continuation of economic liberalization will be in the hands of the new, probably military rulers. They may well recognize that the volume of foreign assistance has grown to such a degree that it cannot be disregarded, and thus the development program scrapped. The present level of foreign support is predicated on the continuity of the reform measures as well as political stability.

The institutional changes wrought by the military, the party structure, and the constitution with its array of people's councils are likely to remain in some form so long as the present generation of the military continues in leadership roles. Too much propaganda and too many egos are involved to have the reforms lightly altered in any significant way. They are unlikely to be dismantled quickly, although prudence and conciliation could prompt new leadership to delegate more power to minority regions. Even if steps were taken in this direction, they would probably be too small to be effective.

It is not clear whether a solution to Burma's enduring problems lies in the immediate future. If there is one, it will be Burmese in essence; if there is none, then the Burmese will handle the absence of a solution in a very Burmese manner. A solution cannot be imposed by outside powers or interests, neither by the logic of development planning nor by abstract ideologies. The Burmese have shown themselves to be adaptable and pragmatic, but in their own way and at their own pace. There is no reason to believe that the future will be any different.

If Burma does not in the near term begin to reach the potential that its rich land and diverse and talented people so clearly demonstrate, it still remains a golden land, full of promise, a *suvannaphumi* awaiting realization for the benefit of all its people.

Dramatis Personae

Aung Gyi, (Brigadier) – Born 1918 in Prome District of a Sino-Burmese family. Spent some of his early years in China. Participated in anti-British activity before World War II and anti-Japanese action later. 2d. Lt., 4th Burma Rifles. In 1947, secretary-general, Burma Socialist party. Member, 1947, Constituent Assembly. In 1948, parliamentary secretary to the minister of defense. In 1950, colonel, later brigadier. Key figure in caretaker government, 1958–1960, and heir apparent to Ne Win in 1962. Ousted from office, January 1963, later jailed and then released. Now retired.

Aung San, (General) – 1916–1947. Father of independent Burma. Born 1916 in Magwe District. Key leader of the 1936 Rangoon University student strike, and in 1939 became secretary-general of the Dobama Asiayone. Arrested by the British in 1939 and later released. Joined the Japanese as leader of the Thirty Comrades. Returned to Burma with the Japanese and became minister of defense in 1943 under the Ba Maw government. Joined the anti-Japanese movement and after World War II negotiated with British for independence and with the minorities for a unified Burma at Panglong in 1947. Assassinated under the orders of U Saw, July 1947.

Ba Maw, (Dr.) – Born 1897 in Amherst District, perhaps partly Armenian. M.A., 1917, Rangoon College; also educated in England and called to the bar. Ph.D., University of Bordeaux. Defense counsel for Saya San. Minister of education, 1934. Founded Sinyetha party, 1936. Arrested on sedition charges, 1940, by British, and then escaped. Named *adipadi* ("head of state") by Japanese. Arrested and imprisoned for one year following war. Perhaps the leading intellectual of his period. Deceased.

Ba Nyein, (U) – Born 1916 at Monywa. Graduated Rangoon University, 1937, in economics. Joined civil service before World War II and then participated in Japanese administration. In 1950, left the Burma Socialist party and helped found the Burma Workers and Peasants' party. A devout Marxist, he became economic adviser to Ne Win after the 1962 coup and then fell out of favor as economic policies failed in late 1960s.

Ba Swe, (U) – Born 1915 at Tavoy. Secretary-general, Rangoon University Student Union, 1937–1938; later president. Founder of National Revolutionary party against the British, 1940–1944. Leader of the Burma Socialist party and the AFPFL. Elected to Parliament, 1951–1952; minister of defense, 1952; and minister of mines, 1953. Prime minister, 1956–1957; also deputy prime minister. Secretary-general of the Socialist party, vice-president of AFPFL. Jailed after 1962 coup; later released. Now in retirement.

Kodaw Hmaing, (Thakin) – Born 1875, educated in Buddhist monasteries. Active in Dobama Asiayone; leading nationalist and leftist; author of eighty plays and fifty books. Winner of International Stalin Prize, 1954. Deceased.

Kyaw Nyein, (U) – Born 1915 at Pyinmana. Educated at Mandalay College and University of Rangoon; active in anti-British activities at the university. Secretary-general, AFPFL; founding member and on executive committee, Burma Socialist party. Minister of cooperatives, acting foreign minister, minister of industries, and deputy prime minister during civilian governments. Retired.

Ne Win, (General) – Born 1911 near Prome as Shu Maung, Sino-Burman. Attended University of Rangoon. Member of Thirty Comrades; deputy to Aung San during World War II. Lt. Col., Burma army, 1945. Member, AFPFL. Deputy commander, Burma army, 1948; commander, 1949. Also minister of defense, deputy prime minister in civilian governments. Prime minister in caretaker government, 1958–1960. Chairman, Revolutionary Council, 1962–1974. President of the Socialist Republic, 1974 to 1981. Chairman, BSPP, 1962 to present.

Nu, (U) – Born 1907 at Wakema. Educated at the University of Rangoon. President, Rangoon University Student Union, 1935–1936. Founded Nagani Book Club, treasurer of Dobama Asiayone. Minister of foreign affairs under Japanese and later minister of information. President of the AFPFL after Aung San. President of the Constituent Assembly, 1947. Prime minister for most of civilian period. Formed Pyidaungsu party, 1960. After coup, jailed and later released. Left Burma to lead military campaign against Ne Win from Thailand. After this failed, sought exile in India. Returned to Burma under the amnesty of 1980. Now translating Buddhist texts. Playwright and author.

San Yu, (General) – Born 1918 in Prome District of Sino-Burman parents. Attended Rangoon Medical College. Vice-chief of staff (army) from 1963. Member, Revolutionary Council from 1962. Deputy prime minister in 1971. Minister of defense and chief of staff, Burma Defense Services. Secretary, BSPP. President, Socialist Republic, November 1981–

Saw, (U) – 1900–1948. Born in Tharrawaddy. Pleader and legislator. Formed Myochit party. Jailed for sedition in 1933. Minister, 1939. Prime minister, 1940–1942. Interned during war by British. Arrested for Aung San's assassination, tried, hanged May 1948.

Soe, (Thakin) – Born 1910 in Moulmein. Member, Dobama Asiayone. One of the organizers of the Burma Communist party. In 1946, split with the BCP and founded the Red Flag Communist party, a Trotskyist group. In revolt from 1946 until November 1970 when he was captured. Released from prison under 1980 amnesty.

Than Tun, (Thakin) – 1911 or 1915–1968. Attended Teacher Training College. Active in Dobama Asiayone. Organized Burma Communist party. First secretary of AFPFL. Resigned in 1946. In rebellion from 1948 until September 1968 when he was assassinated by his own men.

Thein Pe Myint, (Thakin) – Born 1914 Lower Chindwin District. Attended Mandalay Intermediate College, graduated Rangoon University. Active in Dobama Asiayone. Secretary, Burma Communist party, 1943. Journalist and author of *Tet Pongyi* [Modern monk], *What Happened in Burma,* and other books. Burma's leading writer.

Tin, (Thakin) – Born 1903. Active in Dobama Asiayone. Elected to Parliament in 1951–1952 elections. Minister of agriculture and forests. Since 1941, leader of the All-Burma Peasants' Organization, an important mass organization of the AFPFL. Also on Presidium of the Burma Socialist party.

APPENDIX B

Statistics on Burma

TABLE 1
Burmese Population Statistics

_____

Area   676,552 square kilometers
Population   33.59 million (1979)
Density   50 persons per square kilometer
                                        179 persons per square kilometer of arable
                                        land

Crude Birth Rate (per 1000)   36.8   (1980)[1]/
Crude Death Rate (per 1000)   10.8   (1980)[1]/
Infant Mortality (per 1000 live births) 51.6[1]/
Population Increase   2.2%[1]/
Life Expectancy at Birth   53   (1978)
Per Capita Gross National Product $150 (1978)
Income Distribution   Percent of national income (1972) in highest 20%--40%
                        Percent of national income (1972) in lowest 20%-- 8%

_____

Note:

1. Probably underestimated

130

TABLE 2
Population Density and Literacy by Administrative Unit

Administrative Unit	Population (000, 1975)	Density (per sq. mile)	Literacy (% 1973)	
			male	female
Rangoon Division	3,331[1] /	813	87.5	74.1
Pegu Division	3,318	208	84.4	65.0
Irrawaddy Division	4,338	307	82.0	64.9
Magwe Division	2,753	152	86.5	56.5
Mandalay Division	3,825	257	88.0	68.9
Sagaing Division	3,252	85	80.0	46.6
Tenasserim Division	749	42	74.1	57.4
Shan State	3,313	44	48.0	30.1
Kachin State	765	19	62.5	45.6
Chin State	281(1974)	22	48.6	24.5
Arakan State	1,786	110	59.1	35.8
Kayah State	130	23	50.5	33.4
Mon State	1,371	275	69.3	51.6
Karen State	895	56	47.8	33.9

Note:
1. Including Rangoon City

TABLE 3
Education

	1953	1963	1979
Primary Schools	4,795	13,284	23,099
Primary School Students (000)	641.6	1,850.6	3,731.2
Middle Schools	210	651	1,302
Middle School Students (000)	67.7	225.4	754.1
High Schools	137	322	596
High School Students (000)	20.5	43.6	170.7
University/College Students (000)	n.a.	18.9	64.6[1] /

Note:
1. Excluding correspondence course students

TABLE 4
Agriculture

	Years			
	1940/41	1961/62	1974/75	1979/80
Acreage under				
production (000)	18,686	19,013	23,473	24,409[1]
Paddy acreage (000)	12,200[2]	11,359	12,793	12,777
Paddy production (000 tons)	7,800[2]	6,726	8,448	10,493
Paddy yields/acre (in 46 lb. baskets)	30.5	31.16	34.09	42.8
Exports - rice (000 tons)	3,123	1,676	166	700[3]
Rice exports (000 U.S. $)	46.6[2]	87.0	40.0	157.6
Irrigated area (000 acres)	1,562	1,324	2,412	2,550[1]

Notes:

1. 1979
2. 1939
3. Estimate

TABLE 5
Public Capital Expenditures

	(Percent)				
	1964/65	1969/70	1971/72	1975/76	1978/79[1]
Agriculture	11.3	6.2	8.5	14.4	6.6
Livestock & Fishery	0.5	0.3	0.3	1.6	5.5
Forestry	1.9	1.2	1.7	2.8	6.9
Mining	4.4	4.7	5.4	16.2	10.3
Processing & Manufacturing	13.4	44.9	29.1	14.7	36.2
Power	2.9	3.1	6.4	7.0	7.6
Construction	15.8	5.8	5.1	3.7	2.1
Transport & Communications	14.0	13.2	9.5	17.9	14.6
Trade	6.7	1.0	1.9	2.3	1.3
Social Services	3.1	4.1	2.6	4.4	2.4
Financial Institutions	0.1	0.1	3.9	0.3	0.1
Others	25.9	15.4	25.6	14.7	6.4
Total	100.0	100.0	100.0	100.0	100.0

Source: Planning Department, Ministry of Planning and Finance.
         Report to the Pyithu Hluttaw 1979/80.

1/ Revised Estimate.

TABLE 6
Production of the Processing and Manufacturing
Sector by Ownership (Lakh Kyat – Constant 1969/70 Prices)

	State	Private/Coop	Total	State as % of total
1961/62	12,741	31,809	44,550	28.6
1962/63	16,128	34,911	51,039	31.6
1964/65	20,772	30,264	51,036	40.7
1968/69	20,646	31,889	52,535	39.3
1970/71	23,285	31,887	55,172	42.2
1974/75[1]	18,376	32,789	51,165	35.9
1976/77[2]	25,847	33,193	59,040	43.8
1977/78[2]	27,542	35,919	63,461	43.4
1978/79 (Provisional)	29,509	40,111	69,620	42.4

Sources: Report to the Hluttaw 1977/78.
Report to the Hluttaw 1978/79.
Report to the Hluttaw 1979/80

1 / Foodstuffs and beverage production was 37.7% of state sector,
80.7% of the private sector, and 62.7% of the combined state, private, and cooperative
sectors in 1975/76.
2 / In 1976/77, the state share of processing and manufacturing was 43.8%, cooperatives 3.4%,
and the private sector 52.8%

Suggested Reading

Too little literature has been written on Burma in any language. All of the published books in English on Burma since the eighteenth century from nongovernmental sources would fill a rather modest bookcase. Yet there are highly significant works that contribute to our knowledge of Burma and some that also have considerable charm.

The reader with a taste for history might well delve into the reports of official missions to the Burman court. Three that might be mentioned are:

Henry Yule. *A Narrative of the Mission to the Court of Ava in 1855.* London, 1856; Reprint ed., Kuala Lumpur: Oxford University Press, 1968.
John Crawfurd. *Journal of an Embassy from the Governor-General of India to the Court of Ava.* 2 vols. London, 1834.
Michael Symes. *An Account of an Embassy to the Kingdom of Ava Sent by the Governor-General of India in the Year 1795.* London, 1800.

Valuable sources for detailed, although dated, data on particular areas of Burma are the district gazetteers published as a series over many years in Rangoon. Many of them have been reprinted by various Burmese governments. The most ambitious and fascinating study is Sir James George Scott's *Gazetteer of Upper Burma and the Shan States* (Rangoon, 1900) in five volumes. It contains a wealth of historical, economic, and anthropological data that are invaluable for study of the early period. The reader may also wish to turn to selected articles in the *Journal of the Burma Research Society,* published since 1910. Selected articles were republished in two volumes in 1960.

BURMESE LIFE

The most important, and still the most charming, description of Burman life and customs is Shway Yoe (pseudonym for Sir J. George Scott), *The Burman: His Life and Notions* (London, 1883; ed., London: Macmillan, 1910; Reprint ed. in paperback, New York: Norton Library, 1963). Another important description of upper-class Burmese life is by a Mon woman who later married into the Shan *sawbwa's* family: Mi Mi Khaing, *Burmese Family* (London, 1946; Reprint ed., Calcutta: Orient Longmans, 1956). Mention should also be made of the sympathetic, if paternalistic, works of W. Fielding Hall, which include: *The Soul of a People* (London, 1898); and *A People at School* (London: Macmillan, 1906).

GENERAL HISTORY

Several general histories of Burma focus on the pre–contemporary period. These include:

Father Sangermano. *A Description of the Burmese Empire*. Rome, 1833. Reprint ed., London: Susil Gupta, 1966. The earliest history of Burma in Western languages.

G. E. Harvey. *History of Burma*. London: Longmans, Green, 1925.

Sir Arthur P. Phayre. *History of Burma*. London: 1883. Reprint ed., London: Susil Gupta, 1967.

D.G.E. Hall. *Burma*. London: Hutchinson's University Library, 1950.

Htin Aung. *A History of Burma*. New York: Columbia University Press, 1967.

D.G.E. Hall. *A History of Southeast Asia*. London: Macmillan, 1955. A general study with extensive chapters on Burma.

No mention of Burmese history would be complete without reference to a specialized and monumental work: Gordon H. Luce, *Old Burma-Early Pagan*, Artibus Asiae supplementum 25 (Locust Valley, N.Y.: J. J. Augustin, 1969–70). Three volumes. Not for the general reader.

For the modern period, the following are recommended:

John Cady. *A History of Modern Burma*. Ithaca, N.Y.: Cornell University Press, 1958.

Hugh Tinker. *The Union of Burma*. London: Oxford University Press, 1957.

Frank N. Trager. *Burma: From Kingdom to Republic*. New York: Frederick A. Praeger, 1966.

Dorothy Woodman. *The Making of Burma*. London: Cresset Press, 1962.

ANTHROPOLOGICAL STUDIES

There have been comparatively few major anthropological studies of any of the Burmese ethnic groups, although there are quite a few descriptive accounts. More recent works include the following:

E. R. Leach. *Political Systems of Highland Burma. A Study of Kachin Social Structure.* Cambridge, Mass.: Harvard University Press, 1954. A classic in the field of anthropology and the most important on the Kachin.

F. K. Lehman. *The Structure of Chin Society. A Tribal People of Burma Adapted to a Non-Western Civilization.* Urbana: University of Illinois, 1963. The most detailed study of the Chin.

E. Michael Mendelson. *Sangha and State in Burma. A Study of Monastic Sectarianism and Leadership.* Ed. by John P. Ferguson. Ithaca, N.Y.: Cornell University Press, 1975. A monumental study.

Manning Nash. *The Golden Road to Modernity. Village Life in Contemporary Burma.*
New York: John Wiley, 1965. The only detailed contemporary account of
Burman life at the village level.

Melford E. Spiro. *Buddhism and Society. A Great Tradition and Its Burmese
Vicissitudes.* New York: Harper and Row, 1970. An important work.

Melford E. Spiro. *Burmese Supernaturalism.* Englewood Cliffs, N.J.: Prentice Hall,
1967. The only study of this important subject.

Melford E. Spiro. *Kinship and Marriage in Burma: A Cultural and Psychodynamic
Analysis.* Berkeley: University of California Press, 1977. Another important
study.

An extremely good survey of mainland Southeast Asia from an an-
thropological viewpoint that includes extensive material on Burma is Charles F.
Keyes, *The Golden Peninsula. Culture and Adaptation in Mainland Southeast Asia.*
New York: Macmillan, 1977.

POLITICAL AND ECONOMIC STUDIES

A number of studies deal with politics or economics, generally focusing on
specific periods. The following partial list is recommended:

Michael Adas. *The Burmese Delta.* Madison: University of Wisconsin Press, 1974.
A study of the development of the Irrawaddy Delta.

J. Russell Andrus. *Burmese Economic Life.* Stanford: Stanford University Press,
1948. A major study of the prewar period.

Ba Maw. *Breakthrough in Burma. Memoirs of a Revolution.* New Haven, Conn.:
Yale University Press, 1968. Memoirs of a leading prewar politician.

Richard Butwell. *U Nu of Burma.* Stanford: Stanford University Press, 1963. Bi-
ography of a leading Burmese politician.

Siok-hwa Cheng. *The Rice Economy of Burma 1852–1940.* Kuala Lumpur: University of Malaya Press, 1968. An important study of a specialized subject.

John LeRoy Christian. *Modern Burma.* New York: Institute of Pacific Relations,
1942. An important work on the prewar period.

J. S. Furnivall. *An Introduction to the Political Economy of Burma.* Rangoon: People's Literature Committee and House, 1957a. An important study by an ex-
colonial officer.

J. S. Furnivall. *Colonial Policy and Practice.* Cambridge: Cambridge University
Press, 1957b. A classic study of Burma and the Netherlands East Indies.

F. K. Lehman, ed. *Burma Under Military Rule. A Kaleidoscope of Views.* Singapore:
Institute of Southeast Asian Studies, 1981. A symposium on the military
period in Burma.

Moshe Lissak. *Military Roles in Modernization. Civil-Military Relations in Thailand
and Burma.* Beverly Hills, Calif.: Sage Publications, 1976. An important
comparative study of the Burmese military.

Maung Maung. *Burma and General Ne Win.* London: Asia Publishing House,
1969. A sympathetic portrait by a leading figure in the military regime.

U Nu. *U Nu, Saturday's Son.* New Haven, Conn.: Yale University Press, 1975. Memoirs of the former prime minister.

Lucian Pye. *Politics, Personality, and Nation-Building: Burma's Search for Identity.* New Haven, Conn.: Yale University Press, 1962. An important study of Burmese political and social structure.

E. Sarkisyanz. *Buddhist Backgrounds of the Burmese Revolution.* The Hague: Martinus Nijhoff, 1965. A major and specialized work on the relationships between Buddhism and politics and economics.

Josef Silverstein. *Burma. Military Rule and the Politics of Stagnation.* Ithaca, N.Y.: Cornell University Press, 1977. One of the two studies of the military period in Burma.

Josef Silverstein. *Burmese Politics. The Dilemma of National Unity.* New Brunswick, N.J.: Rutgers University Press, 1980. A study of the history of minority problems, stressing the preindependence period.

Donald Eugene Smith. *Religion and Politics in Burma.* Princeton, N.J.: Princeton University Press, 1965. A good study of an important problem, less detailed than Sarkisyanz.

David I. Steinberg. *Burma's Road Toward Development: Growth and Ideology Under Military Rule.* Boulder: Westview Press, 1981. A political and economic study of the military period.

Frank N. Trager. *Building a Welfare State in Burma 1948-1956.* New York: Institute of Pacific Relations, 1958. A study of the early period of Burmese economic planning.

Louis Walinsky. *Economic Development in Burma 1951-1960.* New York: Twentieth Century Fund, 1962. The most detailed study of economic development during the civilian period.

OTHER WORKS

Several other works, although not centered on Burma, are important to include with materials on Burma:

G. Coedes. *The Indianized States of Southeast Asia.* Ed. by Walter F. Vella and trans. by Susan Brown Lowing. Honolulu: East West Center Press, 1968 (Translation of the 1964 French edition.) A classic work on early Southeast Asian history.

Charles F. Keyes, ed. *Ethnic Adaptation and Identity. The Karen on the Thai Frontier with Burma.* Philadelphia: Institute for the Study of Human Issues, 1979. The most sophisticated study of the Karen with much material on the Karen in Burma.

Peter Kunstadter, ed. *Southeast Asian Tribes, Minorities, and Nations.* 2 vols. Princeton: Princeton University Press, 1967. Important articles on the Burmese minorities in volume 1.

Frank M. Lebar, Gerald C. Hickey, John K. Musgrave. *Ethnic Groups of Mainland Southeast Asia.* New Haven: Human Relations Area Files Press, 1964. An encyclopedia of information on minorities by group, containing much on Burmese minorities.

Glossary

Burman: A member of Burma's dominant ethnolinguistic group speaking Burmese as the native language and wearing the dress associated with that group.

Burmese: A citizen of the Union of Burma of any ethnolinguistic group.

Burma Proper: Central Burma exclusive of the constituent states; i.e., all the divisions of Burma.

Lower Burma: British Burma before 1885. Generally limited to Irrawaddy, Rangoon, Pegu, Arakan, and Tenasserim divisions and (since 1974) the Mon and Arakan states.

Upper Burma: Burma under the Mandalay monarchy after the Second (1852) but before the Third Anglo-Burmese War (1885–1886). Today generally equated with Mandalay, Sagaing, and Magwe divisions.

AFPFL: Anti-Fascist People's Freedom League; a political party that split into "Clean" (U Nu dominated) and "Stable" (U Ba Swe, U Kyaw Nyein dominated) factions.

Asiayone: "Organization."

Awza: "Power."

BCP: Burma Communist party, called the White Flag Communists.

BSPP: Burma Socialist Programme party, also called the Lanzin party.

Chettyar: Indian moneylending caste from Madras.

Delta: Irrawaddy Delta.

Dobama Asiayone: "We Burmans Association."

DSI: Defense Services Institute, a military-run conglomerate.

GDP: Gross domestic product.

GNP: Gross national product.

Hluttaw: Pyithu Hluttaw, or People's Assembly. Formerly the highest administrative body under the Burman monarchs.

Kan: Karma, the belief that one's present and future lives are determined by actions in previous incarnations.

KMT: Kuomintang, or Chinese Nationalist party, whose anti-Communist forces retreated into Burma.

KNDO: Karen National Defense Organization.

Lanzin party: Myanma Lanzin party, or Burma Socialist Programme party (BSPP).

Longyi: Sarong, worn by both men and women.

Nat: Burmese spirit.

NUF: National Unity Front, left-wing political party.

Paddy: Unmilled rice.

PDP: Parliamentary Democracy party.

Pon: "Glory."

PVO: People's Volunteer Organization.

Pyidaungsu party: Union party, led by U Nu. Formerly called the Clean AFPFL.

Sangha: Buddhist monkhood and organization.

Sawbwa: Shan local hereditary ruler, maharaja.

Saya: "Teacher."

Sinyetha: "Poor Man's party," a preindependence political force.

SRUB: Socialist Republic of the Union of Burma.

Tatmadaw: The armed forces of Burma.

Thakin: "Lord," or "master," a title used to address the British, later adopted by the nationalist leaders of the 1930s; equivalent to "sahib" in India.

U: Burmese for "uncle"; a term of respect, equivalent to "Mr."

YMBA: Young Men's Buddhist Association.

Yoma: Hills, literally "central bone."

Burmese Names: There are no surnames in Burma. Names of mature men have *U* or a title as a prefix; e.g., U Nu, Bogyoke ("General") Ne Win, Thakin Kodaw Hmaing. Other prefixes are *ko,* "elder brother," used among equals by males; *maung,* "younger brother," used for inferiors and younger males; *daw,* "aunt," similar to *U; ma,* "younger sister," similiar to *maung.*

A Note on Burmese Pronunciation: The Burmese sound system is composed of thirty-one consonants and nine vowels. It has four tones. *U* is pronounced "oo," not "you"; *ky* is "j." The final *t* in *nat* and *tatmadaw* is a glottal stop and is not articulated; *ng* endings, as in *maung,* nasalize the preceding vowel.

Measurements and Exchange Rates

Kyat: Burmese currency. On independence equal in value to the Indian rupee. When followed by figures in the text, it is indicated as *K,* and the rupee is noted as *R.* The kyat is divided into 100 pyas.

Lakh: 100,000 rupees.

Crore: 10,000,000 rupees.

Viss: 3.6 pounds.

Basket: Paddy = 46 pounds. Rice = 75 pounds.

Burmese Fiscal Years: Until 1973, October 1–September 30; after 1973, April 1–March 31. In the text, Burmese fiscal years are always noted with a slash; e.g., 1977/78 is fiscal year April 1, 1977–March 31, 1978. A dash in the text indicates the period between those two calender years; e.g., 1977–1978 includes all of 1977 and 1978.

Burmese Kyat–U.S. Dollar Exchange Rates:

1948–December 1971	U.S.$1.00–K4.76
1971–1972	U.S.$1.00–K5.35
1973–January 1975	U.S.$1.00–K4.81
1975–1980	U.S.$1.00–K6.62

All these rates are official rates. Black market rates vary widely.

Index

143